The Breakthrough Effect

INSPIRATION & EQUIPPING
FOR YOUR BREAKTHROUGH
FROM 17 EXTRAORDINARY WOMEN

Quantity order requests can be emailed to:
Kimberly@thefewwomen.com

The Breakthrough Effect
Publishing Coordinator: Kimberly Joy Krueger

Contributing Authors (in order): Kimberly Joy Krueger, Luanne Nelson, Julissa Moreno, Jacqueline Jaske, Amy Sikkema, Danelle Skinner, Brenda Weber, Maria Notch, Reji Laberje, Angie Riemer, Victoria Dreckman, Traci Weldie, Jennifer Buchholz, Heather Taylor, Joni Jones, Lisa Murphy, Kristina Ward

Contributing Editors: Reji Laberje, Bucket List to Bookshelf, www.bucketlisttobookshelf.com
Associate Editors: Amy Oaks and Kimberly Joy Krueger
Cover Design: Nada Orlic, Nada Orlic Design, and Reji Laberje
Interior Layout: Reji Laberje

ISBN-13: 978-1-949494-05-1

Categories:
Religion & Spirituality/Christian Books & Bibles/Literature &
    Fiction/Collections & Anthologies
Religion & Spirituality/Christian Books & Bibles/Biographies
Biographies & Memoirs/Reference & Collections

FEW International Publications
An Extraordinary Publishing Experience

FEW International Publications is for women authors at all levels who are seeking more from telling their stories than just a printed project. FEW Authors, publishing under four unique lines of books, want to learn and grow through the experience of creating a written work that impacts others and glorifies God.

Extraordinary Women; Extraordinary Stories

http://kimberlyjoykrueger.com/few.php

TABLE OF CONTENTS

God

says

it's time...

Kimberly Joy Krueger, President of FEW and four-time #1 Bestselling author has overcome life's struggles with beauty, dignity, and grace. She has run more than ten 5Ks, half marathons, and full marathons in the years since being hit by a car in 2014, but her favorite race is her race with God and she runs it to win! Kimberly helps women to see their true value and reach their God-given potential. Her mission is to empower women to live extraordinary lives and tell their stories. Kimberly says that her greatest accomplishment in life is being a wife, mother to twelve children, and "Noni" to five (perfect) grandchildren. Visit **www.kimberlyjoykrueger.com** for more information on Kimberly and FEW.

Breakthrough

❧ ❧   ❧ ❧

1

FROM BREAKDOWN TO BREAKTHROUGH

Kimberly Joy Krueger

"He brought me up from a desolate pit, out of the muddy clay, and set my feet on a rock, making my steps secure."

❧ *Psalm 40:2*

I was twenty-one years old, married with three kids, and well on my way to becoming a "baby-making machine," which was ok by me! A big, happy family was all I ever wanted. So why did I feel such an ache … like something really important really big was missing?

While growing up, I knew of God. I even asked Jesus into my heart as a little girl, but this empty feeling told me that knowing *about* God wasn't enough. It was almost an insecure or unsafe feeling—like I wasn't really sure if God had my back. Was I safe in His care like so many of the Bible heroes were? I couldn't really answer that. So, one day, when I just couldn't deal with the achy, empty, unsure feeling anymore, I prayed....

"Lord, I know about you. I even know lots of Bible stories, but I also know I am not living for You. I don't really even know what that means. If You show me how, I will live for You and I will serve You. So, I give you my life—to do with what you want. Amen. "

I quickly offered *every* part of my life to God, including my womb. I wanted the lives God chose to bring into this world through me to be my offering back to Him. I promised God I would raise them to love and serve Him. I went on to have eight more children, totaling eleven, in order to love them and raise them up for God and His purposes. I felt called to offer my life to God in this way and was excited and a little (okay a lot) scared to do it. I dreamed of my whole family one day loving and serving God together. It was all I wanted.

Shortly after I prayed that prayer, someone I respected greatly told me that I was a leader. He said he saw leadership in me, and that there was a call on my life for God and His Kingdom.

I was told I had a destiny.

Me? Imagine that! (I couldn't.) A Leader? Wow. I *wanted* it to be true. Oh, I *hoped* it was true. But I wasn't quite ready to believe it was true! After all, it was ME we were talking about. The me who seemed to screw everything up. The me who seemed to screw everything up. The me who was always in trouble as a teen which was solidified by the fact that I became a mother at sixteen.

The sad part about my response was that I was already a mother of three when he told me this and I didn't see myself as a leader. Not only was I already a leader, but I had three little followers who did everything I did and said everything I said! I also did not understand that God's Word says that just by being a follower of Christ, we are leaders in this world. I was clueless.

Clueless or not, a flame was fanned in my heart—the flame of destiny! I was destined to do things for God and His Kingdom! Good things. Eternal things. My life had greater purpose than I ever imagined. All of my feelings of longing and worthlessness were finally conquered by . . . purpose!

Because I'm a dreamer, I began to imagine what leadership might look like one day. It was so exciting! I had led such a painful, defeated life already, even at such a young age, that envisioning a victorious future was empowering. In addition to being a teen mom, I came from a broken home, my relationships were very toxic, I lived in rebellion during my teenage years, and I experienced abuse by my first serious boyfriend. I had a lot of shame and regret for such a young woman, so the idea of a life of meaning thrilled me. Even though I had no idea how or when it would happen, I set my hopes on it. A door of possibility had been opened to me. I would go to church and overflow with joy; on fire for God and full of expectation for my future destiny. All things were possible! (Inside the church walls, anyway.)

And then I would go home....

Things at home were not good. We needed a breakthrough. I had no clue the number of breakthroughs we were yet to need. At the time, I really didn't even understand what a breakthrough was or what it would look like.

breakthrough

[breyk-throo]

noun

1. an act or instance of removing or surpassing an obstruction or restriction; the overcoming of a stalemate.

2. any significant or sudden advance, development, achievement, or increase, as in scientific knowledge or diplomacy, that removes a barrier to progress.

Synonyms: Advancement, Enhancement, Refinement
Related Words: Upgrade, Uptrend, Upswing

I realized that all of the related words look *up*, which is where we have to look for our breakthroughs! Now I understand a breakthrough to be a **sudden shift that was years in the making**.

To paint a picture of breakthrough, imagine a seed planted beneath the ground. People see the plant pop out of the ground, but every day before that, they saw nothing happen. Then, life. The plant broke through and there was new life. A lot is going on that can't be seen. So much happens in that dark, cold dirt. In the pit. At that time, I knew my marriage was in a pit - a pit that we had dug together. I tried to make things as good as I could, but we both had brought so much baggage to the marriage. I reasoned that at least my baggage was "Gucci" brand. I further comforted myself with the belief that his was of the "Hefty" variety (the large black ones to be specific). Still, *like attracts like*. We attract what we are. A hot mess will attract a hot mess. Some people are just better at hiding their messes.

Some people are just better at hiding their messes.

Prior to my prayer of dedication to God, at the tender age of twenty-one years old, our three-year marriage almost ended in divorce. My husband would stay out all night on the weekends, go to bars, and get home at 7:00 or 8:00 A.M. the next day. He used drugs with friends to have fun, leaving me home alone with the kids most of the time. When he was home, he was usually "sleeping it off." We fought all the time, and the police were even called several times to break up our fights. I was tired of it. Pregnant with our third child, I told him I wanted a divorce, packed up our young ones, and moved back home with my mom.

He begged me to come home saying he would do anything to save our marriage, so, I gave him another chance. Shortly after his return was when I prayed, and gave myself wholly to God. My decision to go back to church was a turning point for us. We regrouped! I started learning how to be a better wife, and he stopped going to bars, started staying home with me and the kids, and eventually we began attending church together. Things did get better . . . for a little while. I even thought my dream of a big, happy family who served God may come true after all.

Then, I discovered that, while I chose a new life with God, he just chose to go *underground* with his old one. He was using drugs behind my back and lying to cover it up. I believed him, until I could not deny it anymore.

Instead of living my dream, I found myself in a pit, and that pit would be my home for a while. Over the next fifteen years of marriage, my pit would have many names.

Fear	Loss	Control
Pain	Bitterness	Selfishness
Suffering	Anger	Self-Pity
Sorrow	Vindictiveness	Unkindness
Loneliness	Impatience	Manipulation
Dishonesty	Doubt	

Yet that pit was actually exactly what this heart needed. It was in that pit where God began to develop me. Circumstances don't make us who we are, they reveal who we are. My pit revealed the ugliness in me . . . and the more that was revealed, the more desperate I became—desperate for God and desperate for a breakthrough.

Desperation has been a blessing in my life. Turning to God in my desperation is why I am who I am today. It was there, desperate and at my lowest place in that pit, where God fostered and confirmed my dream that I would one day make an impact for His Kingdom. I longed for this; for Him to use our mess to help someone else . . . so that my sadness and suffering would not be wasted.

There were many days I wanted to quit. Many days I cried out to God in my frustration, anger, and self-pity. It seemed that God was always asking me to do the hard things, and that my husband got to do the easy things. I had to trust, believe, surrender my anger, forgive, be faithful, and take care of the kids. Meanwhile, my husband got to forget, blow things off, leave all the work to me, and point his finger at me. At least that's how it looked and felt to me. There were many days I would go up to my bedroom and scream into my pillow, so the kids could not hear me. I would cry about how unfair it was. I would ask God why I always had to take the high road and why I had to be the grownup. I wanted to feel young and wild and free, too. Instead, I felt old and trapped and used. Over and over I'd say: *'It's not fair! Why do I have to be the one, God?'*

God, in His wisdom, never answered my question, but He did ask me a question in return. I'll never forget it. It has been seared on my heart like the branding mark of a cattle rancher.

"If it will help *one* person someday, will you do it *one more* day?"

It worked every time. I always said yes. He knew my longing for my mess to become His message and He knew that the hope of helping even one person would be enough to talk me off the ledge. (He had plenty of opportunities to do it, too!)

He knew my longing for my mess to become his message.

I had eleven children *and* I homeschooled them. Their presence and the weight of the responsibility of their educations were both with me 24/7. I made three meals a day for my small army, cleaned the whole house, did all the laundry, paid the bills (which we could hardly afford), planned the meals and grocery shopped (on a shoestring budget), handled all of the doctor and dentist appointments, took them to their extra-curricular activities, and did it all with what was usually only one car. I felt responsible for everything which meant I felt immense guilt for everything that went wrong. I was riddled with insecurities of all sorts about my appearance, my home, my marriage, my abilities, my parenting, and my children's behavior. I constantly compared my life to others' . . . and mine *always* came up short. I hated the kind of impatient, frustrated mother I had become. I held grudges for years and struggled to learn and maintain forgiveness. My husband and I fought daily and he became verbally and physically abusive, which made me feel like I was going crazy. I hid the reality of his behaviors under the misguided belief that it would dishonor my husband to reveal the truth. I lied for him to his boss for fear he would lose his job and we would be out on the streets. I daydreamed about escaping it all, but feared for my children if I did. They would have no one.

During this season of my life, I also experienced some of the deepest grief I've ever known, as I was kicked out of my church. I miscarried twice; one of whom was a son I buried at sixteen weeks gestation. I would also bury my mother who was only forty-six. The final straw was when I watched one of my sons be tried as an adult for felony crimes he committed as a kid.

After years of trying and failing, for all intents and purposes, I was a failure. I had failed at everything I had ever set my hand to.

My marriage failed.
    I failed as a mother.
        We were failing financially.
            I failed to apply God's Word to my life.
            I was a complete disaster.

I could not see how all of this pain and heartache was doing ANY good, least of all developing me into the leader that man once spoke of; a leader who would someday offer hope and help to others. I couldn't even help myself or my own children! I only saw my deep, dark pit. I had

God says a pit is a process

many names for my pit, but my Lord had names for it, too. If you asked me then, I'd say my pit was a punishment. God says a pit is a process.

I saw only destruction; He was rebuilding my life.
I saw a pit of temptation; it was only a test.
I saw a pile of rubble; He was laying a new foundation.
I saw a pit of denial; He was where the truth set me free.
I saw doubt and unbelief; He was teaching me to trust.
I saw my broken-heart; He was teaching this heart how to love.
I saw only failure; He was raising an overcomer.
I saw abandonment and loneliness; He never left my side.
I saw anger and bitterness; He was teaching me to forgive.
I thought I was unlovable; He introduced me to Love, Himself.
I saw myself as dirty; He was cleansing me there.
I saw my guilt and shame; He assured me He paid it all.
I saw needless suffering; He was turning my pain into gain.
I saw all of my weakness; He taught me to draw from His strength.
I saw blame and pity; He taught me to own my choices.
I saw a pit of despair; He renewed my hope.

I thought it was going to be the death of me, but it was the place my real life in Christ began. I saw wounds meant to break me become the very places He chose to make me like Him.

That pit was actually exactly what this heart needed. Our pits serve to point us toward God, so He can give us what we *need* to be Overcomers. And I *needed* . . . a lot. I was an unhappy, self-pitying enabler and drill sergeant. Although I didn't have much going for me, I had this—I loved Jesus and I had faith.

I had faith, but I had no practical wisdom for living. I did not possess the tools I needed to fix the mess I was in. In fact, it was my lack of the right tools that got me into the mess I was in. I had no idea what love really was. I didn't know I was a textbook enabler, and I certainly didn't know I was in a control battle with everyone I lived with. I practiced little to no self-control. I had no wisdom for parenting, finances, marriage, or even my own self-care.

I asked God to help me every step of the way. I asked. I sought. I knocked. I went to Bible study. I read books. I listened to sermons. I took parenting classes. I began asking people from our church for help. God met me there. It was He who divinely led me to me to every resource which led to every small breakthrough that ultimately led to the biggest breakthrough of all!

One by one, He led me to the missing links in my life: missing truth, missing people, missing wisdom, missing love, missing grace, and missing hope. If there was a gap, He'd fill it. If I didn't know how to do the right thing, He'd point me to a person who could show me. If a lie from the enemy was keeping me in chains, The Holy Spirit led me to the Truth. If I felt like I was alone, and no one understood, He brought someone who did. I learned so much under the divine guidance of the Counselor (with a capital C).

One by one, He led me to the missing links in my life.

I learned that I needed some professional help, too, and there was no shame in that. My therapist, Cindy, was used mightily by God in many ways. She taught me to take good care of myself by setting boundaries and using self-control. I didn't even believe I had any boundaries until a preacher pointed out that self-control is a fruit of the Spirit. He reasoned that if you have the Spirit in you, then you have self-control in you. Once I believed I had it, I I believed I could use it. And then I learned how to practice it. Like lifting weights, I was building up self-control like a muscle. It was one of many things I would learn over the course of my growth in the Spirit.

I learned that denial is the enemy and that the truth is always my friend. No matter how painful.

I learned that I had so much more power over my life than I thought. I could not control everyone around me, but I could control me. I could choose how I sounded, acted, and whether or not I'd listen to disrespectful talk. I could choose how I looked at life, whether I was going to enjoy it, and whether or not I'd allow others to run roughshod over it.

I learned you can't blame a boundary crasher if you never put up a boundary.

I learned that the best person to solve a problem is the one who created the problem . . . and that I was owning *every* problem under our roof. Since I was outnumbered in my home twelve-to-one, it turned out that a lot less problems had my name on them than I thought, so I re-distributed them . . . *happily*!

I took ownership of the problems I did create. I admitted and apologized to my husband for being an enabler to his addictions and helping to destroy our family. I told him I loved him too much to help him kill himself anymore. I took responsibility for what came out of my mouth instead of trying to tell everyone else what should and shouldn't come out of theirs.

I learned that everyone deserves to be treated with respect, and I hadn't been a very respectful person. So, for a whole year I worked on being a respectful person. A *whole* year.

I learned empathy and new ways of communicating with the ones I love. I learned that love always gives the person the chance to go higher; it never helps keep them in the dirt

I learned to build up more and tear down less

I learned that I needed older, wiser women in my life; I learned that when it comes to close friends, four quarters are better than one hundred pennies.

I learned to be open to growth and not fear the growing pains.

I learned to study the Word and pray. I learned to prophecy and interpret the dreams God gave me.

I learned all of this in the pit I once despised, and now I thank my brilliant God for.

Even with my newfound vision and skill set, I wasn't quite out of the woods yet. The stronger I became, the more my husband unraveled. The better my boundaries, and self-care, and the less he could control me; the more he drank and the angrier he became.

In November of 2007, late one Tuesday night, I told him I was contemplating divorce. He became very angry.

The next evening, I went to work at my part-time job. He came home and began drinking early that night.

He became hostile toward the kids, and then left without telling them where he was going. He drove to my workplace, came in stumbling drunk and harassed, threatened, and embarrassed me. I asked him to leave repeatedly. So did my manager.

He finally left. He went home and picked a fight with our seventeen-year old daughter. When she refused to let him in her room, he kicked down the door and attacked her. My son, who was fifteen years old, stepped in and protected her. My daughter broke away from the scuffle, dialed 911 on her cell phone, which was behind her back, and screamed for her dad to leave her brother alone.

My son eventually pinned his father to the ground as the police came running up the staircase. They arrested him, removed him, and he never stepped foot in our home again. *It was over.*

Not quite the breakthrough I thought I'd get. *Not even close.*

My heart ached for my children as I filed for divorce. Meanwhile, criminal court took its course and the kids and I started over again. We were shell-shocked. My children were devastated, afraid, angry, you name it. It was to be expected. I drew every ounce of strength I could get from God and leaned on Him harder than ever.

I drew every ounce of strength I could get from God and leaned on Him harder than ever.

At one point I was working five jobs to make ends meet. I was receiving little to no child support as their father was in and out of prison and rehab. I struggled as a single mom with ten children ages eighteen months to seventeen years. Even though it was a daunting new life, it was a new life nonetheless and I had new hope! I was getting closer to being able to help others. God sure was writing quite the story.

During that time, I held God to His Word for our needs, big and small. I had to. I needed Him so much! I was overwhelmed by the size of the task. Thank God I had His Word in my heart and knew His promises for me and the kids. I would remind Him often: *'Lord, You said you are my husband and a father to my children. Lord, we need you to be all that You promised. We need you badly. I'm counting on you!'*

When my sons would go toe to toe with me, I would run to my Heavenly Husband and say, "Did you hear how your son just spoke to me? What are you going to do about it?"

He is a good Father. He took action. He did what each one of my boys needed.

When we had a need, I reminded Him what He said about providing. I called on Him to pay the bills, clothe us, and feed us. When I found myself with no vehicle, I even expected Him to supply me with a car.

He supplied. Oh how He supplied! I began getting gift cards sent to me for pedicures and massages. I even opened my van door one day and found a fur coat! There was a note on it that said, "From your Father. You're His Princess."

Oh how He supplied!

He put clothes on our bodies and bread on our doorstep. Literally! Every Monday, for quite a long time, an unmarked white van would drop off stacks of flats loaded with Brownberry Bread – the good kind – English muffins, coffee cake, bagels, and bread. The kids did a happy dance every time! He provided and paid for private school for two of my sons – while I was on state aid. He raised up men to love my sons and mentor them. He put my kids in the right classrooms with the difference-making teachers. He made $6000 of unpaid rent just go away. He made electricity "appear" five days after the electric company shut us down. He provided me with free vehicles. *Free.* Vehicle**S**. Plural! The God of the Old Testament who brought water from a rock and rained bread down from Heaven is the same yesterday, today, and forever.

Finally, after two years of the test of my life – single motherhood, I married the love of my life. Scott was handpicked by God, not to save our family, but to serve it. That is exactly what he did from day one.

The year I married Scott was also the year I turned forty and it became the year that God said, '*It's time.*' It was my time. It was time for me to help that "one person" who kept me from giving up on so many of my desperate days.

By God's grace, I launched into my call as a Coach, Author, and Speaker in 2011 and I've been helping people ever since. I went from that icky, old pit to helping other people get out of theirs.

One day, several years after I began to live my call, I sat down, and I asked God a question.

What *exactly* got me out of my pit? What were the things that brought me breakthrough?

I reasoned that if I could identify them, write them down, and tell others what they were, then I could help them get out of their pits, too. I waited for Him to answer and He did! He showed me the things so clearly!

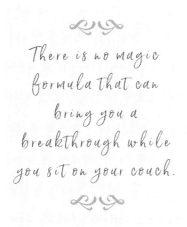

There is no magic formula that can bring you a breakthrough while you sit on your couch.

He showed me five factors and how they worked together to multiply the breakthroughs in my life. He even showed me how they had become a way of life for me through practice, and how they are still at work in my life today. I put them together and created a formula of sorts. There is no magic formula that can bring you a breakthrough while you sit on your couch, but this formula will bring you breakthrough if you partner with God and put these things to work in your life every day.

The first factor He showed me was *faith.* Faith was the foundation that became the catalyst for all of my other breakthroughs. Then, God reminded me of how so many lights went on when I faced the *truth.* Not just the Truth of His Word, but the truth about my husband's addiction and my role as an enabler. Truth is vital for breakthrough. Once I faced the truth, I was also faced with a choice: *'Would I take **personal responsibility** for my part in the problem?'*

My answer was, "Yes," which immediately led to the realization that I needed the **proper tools** if I wanted to right my wrongs and do things better than in the past. I became a student of practical wisdom for life and relationships, ditching my fixed (victim) mind set for a growth mindset. Suddenly I found myself surrounded by *other* growth-minded encouragers who helped form my **solid support** system. Some of these people were brought to me by God, and others were those I sought out, such as my therapist and trusted leaders in the church.

After God showed me how all of these factors were present in my life, He also showed me how they worked together, multiplying each other, to cause a synergy that brought breakthrough after breakthrough in my life.

Crippling insecurity was conquered.

No more self-pity; I'm not a victim anymore.

I've overcome anger and lived a life of forgiveness; no more grudges. I enjoy peaceful and healthy relationships. I've learned to practice patience and use self-control to regulate my emotions. I face the truth, no matter how painful. I've broken through physical barriers, such as asthma and injuries.

No more self-pity; I'm not a victim anymore.

I've started multiple businesses and have written ten books. I speak to audiences on leadership and a variety of other topics to diverse groups, despite the fact that I am not educated in or experienced for what I'm doing today.

Please believe me when I say that I am not boasting; my story only stands to prove that, *if breakthrough was possible for someone as desperate and messed up as me, then it is possible for you, too.* In the wake of my prayer of declaration, when someone told me that I was a leader, only God knew what it would take to turn me into one.

I was told I had a destiny – you have one, too. You'll probably need a few breakthroughs along the way and these five factors will not fail you. Together, they have done miracles in my life, heart, finances, marriage, family, relationships, and health. I spent years of my life in total defeat. Until. Until God showed me how to put these five factors to work in my life (without me even realizing it at the time)!

It is imperative that you understand, had I *not* put Faith, Truth, Personal Responsibility, Proper Tools, and Solid Support to work for me, I would not be living my destiny today. I am not who I once was, and my life has not been the same since *The God Of Breakthroughs*

brought me out of my pit.

> Psalm 40:2 says, "He brought me up from a desolate pit, out of the muddy clay, and set my feet on a rock, making my steps secure."

If He can do it for me, He can do it for you, and He can do it through this book. *The Breakthrough Effect* was designed, not only to inspire you with real breakthrough stories, but to equip you for your own breakthrough.

Faith

You have to believe. You have to believe God's Word above all else and trust in it. Faith is the foundation for your breakthrough by opening the door for the other four factors to enter your life. And the interesting thing about faith that is unlike any of the other factors in this formula is that in some cases the only thing you may need for your breakthrough is FAITH! The Bible is full of stories where faith led to MIRACLES! But faith is more than just belief. Faith does five things to help you get your breakthrough.

1. FAITH SEES
Faith sees the breakthrough before it happens. If you see it in your mind's eye as a done deal, then your faith is activated!

2. FAITH PRAYS
Don't pray with expectations, pray with expectancy! Prayer is simply reminding God of what He already promised you. What has He promised you?

3. FAITH ACTS
Pastor and Author Mark Batterson said, "Pray like it's all up to God and work like it's all up to you." That is the best way I could possibly describe how your faith and efforts should work together. Allow God to do what only He can do, while you obediently do what He tells you to do.

4. FAITH WAITS
At some point in your faith journey, you will have to wait. Abraham waited. Joseph waited. Moses waited. David waited. Jesus waited. Paul waited. The question isn't will you ever have to wait, it is how will you wait? Waiting is different to God than it is to us. To us, it is gritting your teeth and getting through it, but to God, it is waiting with a good attitude, staying loyal to His Promise.

5. FAITH SPEAKS
2 Corinthians 4:13 says, *"But having the same spirit of faith, according to what is written, 'I believed, therefore I spoke,' we also believe, therefore we also speak."* Paul means to say that our words and our faith should not contradict each other, and if we believe, we will declare it with our mouths. So, get ahold of that promise God made you! Then see it, pray it, act on it, wait for it and speak it out!

LUANNE NELSON is a motivational speaker, ordained minister, #1 Bestselling author, wife, and mother. She studied English Literature at Westminster College in Pennsylvania and Journalism at Marquette University. Her love of Jesus Christ and her enthusiasm for God's Word are apparent in both her writing and her joy-filled street ministries. She has been through many adversities and knows the healing grace of God. Her husband calls her, "a Force you can't ignore!" Luanne was once included as one of the most interesting people in the city in *Milwaukee Magazine*. Her hobbies include gardening, piano composition, photography, and antiquing. She loves her corgi and her husband, Dave.

Breakthrough

2

TRUST HIM

Luanne Nelson

Joyful celebration surrounds the birth of a baby, and this little one's arrival was no exception. Meme and Pappap flew in from Pennsylvania excited to cuddle their very first grandchild. She was born on my birthday, a little more than one year after I was married. Her big blue eyes were alert the moment she was born; she seemed not to miss a thing.

The hospital's nurse was generous in her confidence in me, "Don't worry," she offered, "she's never had a Mom, so she won't be judging you. Just love her."

I did.

I do.

Soft little strawberry blonde curls ringed her perfect face and tickled her neck. I remember taking her to see Disney on Ice when she was three years old. The person peddling peanuts and candy up and down the aisles of the auditorium stopped to offer some pink cotton candy.

Our little girl politely said, "No thank you. I prefer green beans."

At home, she twirled and spun around on her head when she was thinking really hard, giggling because she could read a newspaper upside down. She went to French Immersion School at five and could solve a Rubik's Cube in no time flat at six. Her favorite book was *Good Night, Moon*. She loved bright colors and foggy days. Trips to the art museum were frequent and fun.

Thirteen and a half months later, our second child arrived; a beautiful little brut weighing almost ten pounds. His baby face was bruised and his head was misshapen from the rough ride he had coming into this world. This little one truly had a tough start in life. He had trouble taking his first breath and we almost lost him. We prayed frantically and he choked for a moment before catching his first breath.

He was a quiet baby who loved being wrapped snugly in soft blankets, being closely held. He was not interested in walking and saved his mobility skills for the day he could take off running. Dismantling objects was his favorite thing to do; alarm clocks, tricycles, anything mechanical littered the floors.

His kindergarten teacher called me one day saying she had asked each student the name of their favorite song. His classmates answered the usual, *Twinkle, Twinkle Little Star*, *The Farmer in the Dell*, and so forth. My son's answer? Anything Gershwin or Stevie Wonder.

I snapped photos galore. Shoe boxes filled with photos cluttered the closets next to boxes of crayons, finger paints, and wooden blocks.

Shoe boxes filled with photos cluttered the closets.

Less than two years later, our third child was born. She arrived a few weeks after her due date, apparently completely comfortable where she was with no intention of kicking her way out. She was born talking. I am not kidding you. My doc did a midline incision and, before she was lifted out she was chatty and cooing up pixie dust everywhere.

A sweet child, she liked everyone and everything. Her blue eyes were the size of saucers, giving her a constant look of surprise and wonder. The third child born in three years, she quickly learned how to fend for herself. When this littlest one was thirsty, I was usually busy chasing her big sister and brother and would promise to get her something to drink "in a jiffy!" She taught herself how to shimmy up onto the kitchen counter, turn the water on, put her face under the stream of water, and drink straight from the faucet. Self-sufficiency became her forte. Her stuffed Kanga was her best friend. Although the smallest of the three, she was the noisiest. I can still see her lugging her French horn down the driveway after school. It was nearly her size. She was tenacious, tough, and oh so lovely.

The village's sidewalks unrolled into ribbons of adventure, perfect for afternoon strolls. We didn't have a double stroller, so two of the children would take turns teaming up in the seat part and the third would ride on the canvas roof. I made their baby food from scratch, steaming veggies and fruits on the stovetop. We sketched pictures, finger-painted together, and watched *Mr. Roger's Neighborhood* on TV. We went on field trips to see dinosaurs on water towers and lily pads on ponds. Every museum was our playground.

Their dad slept late and went to work around noon at the family's restaurant. He said taking care of children was a woman's job. I starched and ironed his shirts. I made him pastrami on rye with a slice of swiss and a small splash of mustard when he got home from work at midnight. He was a good man with an old-world heart.

Our children were baptized; I taught them how to pray. My husband did not join in because he was an atheist. This was news to me!

Our children were baptized; I taught them how to pray.

He had told me he was an Episcopalian. We went to the mandatory marriage classes at church before our wedding; I had no inkling he was godless. One sunny summer afternoon, I was bringing cookies and milk to him and our eldest little one, who was about five years old at the time.

Getting closer, I heard her dad saying, "Everything in the Bible is a fairy tale. Don't believe any of it. They are just nice stories."

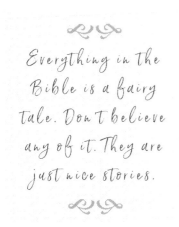

Everything in the Bible is a fairy tale. Don't believe any of it. They are just nice stories.

I was flabbergasted and felt like I had been kicked in the gut. I protested. Don't get me wrong, he really was a kind man with a big heart who loved his children very much. He worked a lot and felt obligated to keep the family business going. His name was on the front door as the third-generation owner. He felt this was his destiny, his lot in life . . . he hated it.

He was so unhappy, and I hoped he would find work he enjoyed. He never did, though, because he felt such a strong allegiance toward keeping the restaurant going. I watched him go through the motions of doing what he thought was right and sacrificing his own precious life in the process.

We rarely saw each other except over those midnight sandwiches and some Sunday afternoons. He was an avid Green Bay Packer fan, so those Sundays were reserved for the game. I took care of the children. I was exhausted and he was miserable. We talked about moving to Colorado away from the family business and starting over. It became clear his allegiance was, and would always be, to the family business.

We divorced. We were just way too tired and unhappy to stay together anymore. When we divorced, I was thirty years old with three children under the age of seven under my wing. I had full custody when we moved closer to where I grew up. Six hundred miles of distance between the misery felt good; I was far away from my former in laws, their restaurant, and that very lonely life. I waived all rights to the lucrative family business during the divorce with this understanding: He would keep the family business . . . and I would keep the children.

During the divorce, my father-in-law told me I "could take care of the children while they were growing up but (he) would have them as adults."

Those words stung and I was confident he was wrong. It was an oppressive lifestyle and I was relieved to get away from it.

I got into a treacherous short-lived relationship with a man who lied about who he really was; I was naïve and ended up in a shelter with the children for victims of domestic abuse a few months later. He apparently had done this to women before me. I was his target; he used my children as leverage. He threatened to have my children taken away if I didn't do this or that. He was in a position where he truly could have made that happen. I was terrified and did whatever he wanted. I had never prayed so hard in my life. I did everything I could to protect and keep my children safe during the chaos. A stranger took my children and me to safety after seeing my blackened eye and bruises on my legs.

Have you ever been at a point in your life where you look around and all you see is wreckage? That's where I was at. One of my children looked at me at the women's shelter and reminded me, "Mom, evil never wins."

I can still see the earnestness in her eyes. Moms will do anything to protect their children, to keep them safe, to keep them in their care. I truly do not think there is a love greater than the love a Mom has for her children.

I was thirty-one years old, scrambling to get back on my feet, with nothing but trust in God to get us through this difficult time. He came through. He always does.

We moved into a cute little rental house a few weeks later. I passed my real estate exam and began selling homes. I also worked part time in the evening raising funds for the local symphony to earn extra money. We were blessed to know a wonderful Italian woman we'd met at church who took care of my little ones while I was working. I was not "street smart"; I was a naïve smarty pants. The devil really

Intelligence doesn't matter when paired with a lack of experience and insight.

likes that combination. Intelligence doesn't matter when paired with lack of experience and insight. I begged God to protect us, and to help me raise my beautiful innocent children. I struggled with finances, usually falling short at the end of each month.

Six hundred miles away, the children's Dad had met a young woman from Chicago while participating in a city pub crawl event. They married a few months later and had a child together shortly thereafter. I have to admit, I cried the day they married. Somewhere in the back of my mind, in my heart, I still believed he would leave the family business and we would start our lives over again in Colorado. We had even talked about it after we were divorced. He explained to me his concern that I would never be accepted back into his family. I realized nothing was ever going to change his mind.

I grew up quickly. I had to. Long gone were the days of sorority teas and Junior League. The privileged life I had while growing up was a distant memory. I daydreamed, reminiscing about an evening many years earlier. I remembered the night my Dad and I were enjoying a car ride together years ago. He asked me what I wanted to be when I grew up.

Joking, I flippantly answered, "A hood ornament on a Rolls Royce."

He was amused and chuckled; he was a kind man with a generous heart.

Later, I learned the ornament is called the Spirit of Ecstasy; an elegantly winged woman that looks like she's experiencing a constant head wind. I was adventurous. I was the smart one. I was the overachiever. I was in National Honor Society, Thespian Society, and was editor of the senior yearbook. I had won a few beauty pageants too. I felt so strong, so smart, and so ready to take on the world back then. When Dad and I arrived home, the conversation continued.

"Be a pharmacist," my Mother advised. "You'll want to have a family. Count pills. Go home at the end of the day," she said.

I dreamed of meeting a family man, marrying, and having a dozen children.

I recalled patting the folds flat on the pleats of my high school uniform's navy and white herringbone skirt. I straightened the shoulder pads in my blue blazer entering the chapel for the last time before high school graduation. We all looked practically the same: a gliding row of navy uniforms with crisp white blouses and Peter Pan collars atop cabled knee socks attached to brown penny loafers. Marching into the pews, we were a small blue army, a gaggle of girls. It seemed like forever ago.

Something caught me completely off-guard after the divorce. My former husband's family decided to act as though I no longer existed. Growing up in Pennsylvania, I saw how the Amish shunned a member who left their community. It was gut wrenching and heartbreaking. I was living that shunning in my own life now. I reasoned I had publicly embarrassed "the family" by divorcing their son. Their name was well-known in the city; their connections were with people they considered to be very important. My former in-laws clearly decided to punish me.

A snow bird living in the southwest during the winter, my former mother-in-law would host an annual party for all of her grandkids when she was back in town for the summer. Christmas, Easter, birthdays, and milestones in my children's lives would come and go without a card or a present in the mail.

The children and I lived on a shoestring.

The aunts and uncles were busy living their lives and were silent, too. Meanwhile, I struggled financially. The children and I lived on a shoestring.

Since moving back to Pennsylvania post-divorce, I drove to Wisconsin in the summertime so the children could spend a few weeks with their dad per the divorce agreement. During one of these trips I took the children to visit their Great Tante, a lively woman in her eighties who was the sister of their late great grandmother, Nana. She loved seeing the children and I was doing my best to keep the lines of communication open however I could.

Tante's grandson stopped by during one of the visits. He and my first husband were cousins in a small, closely-knit family; their grandmothers were sisters. I knew him from family gatherings. He was fun; there was nothing prissy or phony about him. We started dating and married a year later. The children and I moved back to the Midwest.

This marriage never had a chance. Three years into it, a life-changing disaster of epic proportions struck. The phone call came early, before sunrise, one summer morning. The news was devastating. My first husband, the father of my three beautiful children, had taken his own life at the lakefront. We were all devastated beyond words.

Our children, who were nine, eleven and twelve years old, were hardly old enough to even understand death, much less death by one's own hand. There were no words to describe the anguish.

Then, a few weeks later, I suffered a miscarriage.

I was forever entwined in a family who not only was shunning me, now they were blaming me for everything that went wrong. They needed a fall-guy, a scapegoat. After all, if I hadn't divorced their son he would still be alive, right? We are all that powerful, right? My former in-laws and his widow called me on the phone and told me I was not welcome at the funeral home. They said they would send a limousine to pick up the children; I said no.

I took my children to the funeral home.
I stayed with them.
I dried their tears.
I held their hearts in my own.
I sat in constant prayer.

Then, I looked up the name of a Christian family therapist in the Yellow Pages. I was a total mess at thirty-eight years old.

The aftermath was chaotic. A few weeks after their dad's death, his widow claimed he did not have a will. I petitioned his estate in the courts on behalf of our children. Eventually, each child was awarded a small amount of money which cumulatively did not even match my

The aftermath was chaotic.

attorney's fees. I remember writing a check to the attorney for seventy thousand dollars to cover all fees . . . including my second divorce.

I was tired and broken.

33

Often, I felt like I was treading water, armless. There was too much water and not enough air. My former mother- and father-in-law falsely accused me of not letting them see their grandchildren. They sued me for grandparental visitation rights three weeks after their son, the children's Dad, died. This news landed on the front page of the city newspaper. On top of grieving, their sharp tongues ripped through my heart and gutted it. They needed someone to blame for their son's death and I had become their very public whipping post.

My children and I went to grief counseling. We prayed. We had family meetings. We struggled. I was prescribed Xanax. The Xanax was a temporary fix, and I discovered the soothing effects of chardonnay to accompany it. I wanted the sharp edges of the pain dulled. It worked for a while . . . until it didn't work anymore. I had to face the grief *and* all of the suffering that went with it.

When my second husband and I divorced in the dark shadow of that tragedy, the children's teachers mercifully agreed I could keep the children home from school occasionally for mental health days. We worked on purposeful remembering. We put together photo albums and made dozens and dozens of cookies. We lived on a lake, keeping the doors open for their friends. We had dinner together every night and talked about what we learned that day. We always set an extra place in case a friend would drop in so they could just sit right down and join us, which happened often. Some evenings, the dinner place setting remained open and we agreed Jesus Himself was having dinner with us that night.

We planted and harvested three lovely vegetable gardens on the wetlands of our lake property. We went horseback riding. We went to church. We prayed together. I tried to make everything alright.

cb

During a family meeting following their Dad's death, one of the children said, "we're damaged, but we're not ruined."

We're damaged, but we're not ruined.

Each one of my children grew up to be strong, beautiful, and very dear. I did my best with the information I had; I gave to them until I had nothing left to give.

After the youngest one graduated from high school, I moved into a small apartment in the city. I put the few earthly possessions I had left in some boxes and lined them up neatly against my bedroom wall. I shared a bathroom . . . and I shared my pain.

I stayed single for the next ten years. I considered becoming a secular sister. An aunt was a Franciscan nun; I researched the Franciscan lifestyle. I was in a chapel in a Franciscan convent when something extraordinary happened...

Midafternoon sunlight streamed through the stain-glass windows. I was practically alone in the little perpetual adoration chapel. There were a handful of ancient sisters sitting quietly in the surrounding pews. It was quiet and peaceful when I began my silent prayer. *'Dear Jesus Lord, keep my children safe, unbreak their hearts, heal them, heal me . . . please. Please.'*

I nodded off, or at least I thought I did.

When I opened my eyes, I was sitting at a table in an outdoor cafe, a huge umbrella covering the whole table shielding it from the hot summer sun.

I looked up and saw I was having lunch with Jesus. I sat up straight, looking down to make sure I was decently buttoned up.

A beggar approached our table. He was unkempt and dirty, bones protruding through his very soiled tattered garment. I reached to give him some food from my plate.

Jesus commanded, "No, don't do that!"

Startled, I looked up and said to Jesus, "but he's hungry! Didn't You tell us to feed the hungry, give drink to the thirsty, clothe the naked, visit the imprisoned?" I rattled off the corporal works of mercy straight from the Book of Matthew describing His own words from His Sermon on the Mount. Then, I realized I was arguing with our Lord and Master Jesus Himself! I was embarrassed and stopped talking. I felt my face blush.

Jesus said softly, "Do not give him anything."

Totally confused, I asked Him, "I don't understand. Why not?"

Jesus said, "Because that's Satan. If you give him even the smallest piece of anything, he will keep coming back for more and more until there is nothing left of you."

I was trying to do the right thing, the holy thing, following His holy directions and I realized I had it all wrong! Thoughts swirled. I was caught off-guard, out of context, in a different dimension. I looked up at Him and asked, "How do I know when to give and who to give it to?"

"Trust Me," was His answer.

Immediately, I was delivered wide awake back to the wooden pew. I searched the chapel and thought loudly: "Wait! Wait! Don't go! Where are you?"

I realized, at that moment, I had no idea how to trust Him. I had no idea what it *meant* to trust Him. During my life, I had prayed, I performed the works of mercy, I had taught my children how to pray, I had gone to church religiously, and yet here I was – completely baffled.

Time passed. I lived a quiet life downtown, occasionally dating but mostly working. As part of the discernment process in considering religious life, I worked for a while with juvenile delinquents in a semi-secure setting. I was poor and spent many evenings ministering to people living on the streets downtown, praying together with them, spreading hope through His word. A few years later, all of my children, adults in their twenties, were invited to go on an all-paid for luxury cruise with their grandparents and extended family from their father's side. Something strange happened during that cruise; my children came back distant and different. I asked what happened, but was left emptyhanded.

> *"From now on there will be five in one family divided against each other, three against two and two against three. They will be divided, father against son and son against father, mother against daughter and daughter against mother, mother-in-law against daughter-in-law and daughter-in-law against mother-in-law."*
>
> ⌇*Luke 12:52-53 NIV*

I don't think there is a pain greater for a Mom than the agony of being shunned by her own children. Recently, I saw a photo of one of my daughters on Instagram. She was very pregnant. I texted her with a stunned message; she did not respond. She had her baby a few months ago; a beautiful baby girl. I saw the photo on the Internet; my first and only grandchild. I thought I would never stop crying . . .

and praying. I prayed for God to send me someone to pray with and again, He did.

God, in His infinite mercy and generosity sent me a loving man to be my husband and fold his hands with mine in prayer; we've been married for almost fourteen years now. We share our joys and our pain. Sometimes, we fight; we're not perfect, but *always* we pray.

We find solace together in knowing God has all us, including my estranged children, and all of our lives in His hands. He holds our broken hearts in His.

Deep breath.

I've been tracking down some old friends. I found one of my favorite college roommates on Facebook. She offered me more solace than she will ever know. When I told Mary about my kids, she quipped, "Who are we to say we are a better parent than God is?" Her words knocked the breath right out of me.

She's right. God's own children – each and every one of us – are sinners. I am one of them. We are not called to be perfect. We are called to do our best in His care. He does not punish us because we fail; it's in our repentance, our willingness to change – to do better today - that He has mercy on us. His love for us is complete, endless and humanly unfathomable. I know He loves me.

I realize now . . . I trust Him completely. Perhaps because all else has been stripped away except the right to pray and hope. It's a magnificent freefall into His care; knowing that no matter what, everything will be alright in the end . . . and if it's not alright, it's not the end.

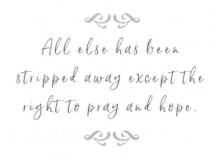

All else has been stripped away except the right to pray and hope.

The late great Eugene O'Neill said it very well. He penned, *"Man is born broken. He lives by mending. The grace of God is glue."*

When I stand back and squint my eyes enough to really see the whole picture – or, at least as much as I am supposed to see, I see clearly that we've always had exactly what we've needed every single day.

In the end of my first marriage, I had family to turn to.

In abuse, I had shelter and protection. In loss, I held my children.

In desperation, I was given a someone to share the gift of prayer.

How could I *not* trust that every situation will be made right for His glory?

It's really true. It's true for each one of us in His care. He has always been with me. He never fails us. Ever. Even in our darkest, most human of moments.

Our Creator, our eternal loving Dad, paints the colors on the flowers and gives the birds their daily food. He loves us more than the flowers and the birds. I am confident He's keeping my maternal arms stashed in a safe place knowing I will need them again to hug all of my children someday. I know the end game. I will not let the adversary steal even one moment of joy in my life. He can't have it any more. I will not give even one little piece of my life away. No. God told me all about that one day . . . over lunch. I get it.

Trust Him.

"And we know that in all things God works for the good of those who love him, who have been called according to his purpose."

↪*Romans 8:28 NIV*

JULISSA MORENO goes by many names, such as, wife, mother, sister, daughter, and granddaughter. She is considered to be a friend, a companion, a partner, a soulmate. Julissa might be described as a women, a Latina, a Puerto Rican, a Brooklynite, and a New Yorker, but – most of all – she is a child of God and her Father in Heaven has kept her and continues keep Julissa and her family with His love and his Grace. Her life has shaped her, trials have strengthened her, and tears have taught her. *"My God has given me the Victory!"*

Breakthrough

3

GOD'S LOVE STORY

Julissa Moreno

*E*veryone has a love story and I, just like many of us, love sharing it. To be quite honest, it's part of the breakthrough. All love stories are special, different, and unique, but what if I told you that your love story began long before you were even a twinkle in your momma's eye. That's quite an amazing and acceptable truth for those who have faith and believe in God.

My love story is just that and more. I had the privilege and advantage to have seen my spouse and family in a dream.

To be honest, I just did not understand what the big deal was. I was only seventeen years old and I was always a dreamer. One thing is certain. This dream stood out more than most, and as I grew older, I wanted it to be true at some point. Before I tell you about the dream, I want you to know that this is just the beginning of my story.

The Dream . . .

I can see hallway stairs and two little girls. Because of their sizes one appears a bit older than the other. They wore pretty, pink, matching coats and had this beautiful, long, dark brown hair. I looked much heavier and wore a light jacket. The girls and I had appeared to be waiting for a man. I can only describe his strong posture and what he wore; I was not able to see his face – just the back of his head. He was dressed in a dark navy-blue business suit. His shoes were polished and had great shine, just like his perfectly round, bald head. He had a nice build and wide, broad shoulders. For a moment he appeared to be their father because they held hands. In the next moment, I bent over to raise the zipper on the littlest girl. I noticed a beautiful rock! This wedding band set was stunning and it shimmered.

I heard a voice say, 'Do not look at the ring for its looks, because its symbol is the foundation of your marriage.'

We then walked out of the house into a truck with two baby car seats and a booster. What I found odd was that both girls were too big for boosters and car seats. We headed to what looked to be our new home. I walked into a room and there was a rose. Attached was a note. "Para mis dos Princesas." I awoke!

This dream was perfect, especially for a girl like me who is a dreamer. I love to paint and imagine the paintings coming to pass. I have been told that God speaks to us through dreams, but at this stage of my life I just saw it as something to desire.

The book of Job says:

"For God may speak in one way, or in another,
Yet man does not perceive it.
In a dream, in a vision of the night,
When deep sleep falls upon men,
While slumbering on the beds,
Then He opens the ears of men,
And seals their instruction".
Job 33:14-16 NKJV

God used this dream to open up my spiritual senses and get my attention. His goal was not met just yet, but I was certainly on a mission to find this man and marry him. Thank God, He is patient with me and didn't throw in the towel after my first attempt.

I became pregnant out of wedlock at the age of nineteen and . . . surprise . . . it was a beautiful little girl I named Sarah Elizabeth. My desire to have this dream come to pass was not far from my mind, but the conviction of not being married bothered me extremely.

I most certainly did not plan to start my family this way! Sarah's father and I did not marry right away either. He did propose, although it was after an ultimatum. We married at city hall, one year after Sarah was born. He was physically and verbally abusive, not to mention a pothead.

Domestic violence was not part of my dream and sharing him with other women (another reality of my husband's actions) was not what I call marriage. So, when and where was I going to have him shave his head and be that business man?

Therapy, marriage counseling, pastoral counseling; I even bought him a car. What was I thinking? I was done!

I called it quits, filed for divorce, and moved out. A year later, he was remorseful. During the year, I would pray he would change and desire to be a family again. I really wanted this dream to be made real, especially since we already had a daughter. I decided to let him back in. A month later, I became pregnant.

There was one moment with a friend of mine, when we had just finished breakfast. While walking afterward, I told her I'd had enough, but I knew that God was going to change him. He was going to have a circumcision of the heart. It made sense to me because of my dream. I had two children from him, and I'd never seen the face in my dream. It had to be him, right?

The Holy Spirit, in that moment, rested on my shoulder. I felt the heat and I was jerked back. My friend was behind me, and through her He said, "How dare you try to make this man fill the shoes of the man of dignity? How do you continuously try to make him wear those clothes."

I was sobbing. I still felt the heat.

"You need to let go of trying to make him into the person God gave you in the dream."

In that moment, I realized that we all have a superwoman complex, thinking we can change people, but it's God's job. He is the supernatural.

After that day, I made it my business to visit the women (three different women who had children by him . . . while we were married). I forgave them. That was another breakthrough journey of forgiveness and healing.

A man with his history would not change without God, and our old, ugly routines were back. I saw him for who he was . . . and who he wasn't . . . and I gave him the boot for good.

Faith Ailynn was born, and although life got harder, she was perfect. Her name was a sure sign of what I needed. I was determined to move forward from my ugly past and focus on my daughters. Love was far from my mind, but not distant enough that it couldn't be reached. I knew my life was not to end with me being a single mom, struggling to make ends meet. God gave me a dream, and somewhere buried in my heart, I was banking on it.

Faith was three months old when their dad was just about out of the picture. He would visit whenever he felt like being dad, and of course, out of love for my daughters, I would allow it. I met this guy named Steven at work and I am not going to lie. The moment I laid eyes on him, this man made me feel like a pig in mud. He had a girlfriend, and I was still dealing with my ex hanging around. It's not the way I would want a relationship to start. My ex-husband continued with his verbally abusive and reckless behavior, just as when we married. The only difference was our living arrangements. I would honestly pray that God would cut him out completely from our lives. He was more of a burden than a parent. Needless say, co-parenting was non-existent.

My conversations with God were like best friends, although—in this relationship—I couldn't hide anything! I didn't see Him as a father, until the day I gave up on trying to control the dream. I cried so much that night because I was exhausted and tired of doing it all alone. I ran into the bathroom at one point so that the girls couldn't hear me sniveling. I just said *'Lord, I need help. We both know I rely on You for everything, and we both know that my girls need more than someone to call dad. They need a father and I need help! This man does not want me nor You. He is not going to change and Yes, I desire to be loved again! There is a guy at work that makes my heart skip and my palms all sweaty. He's hot!'* (God knew I was thinking it, anyway!) *'He smells fantastic, and not to mention, he gives me butterflies. Being around him makes me all giddy inside. I said it! So now that You know what You already know, make this all go away please, because it's not helping me focus. Make my ex get himself together so that maybe he can realize his losses and be a father. Lord, I desire a King David – a man that chases after Your heart because there he will find me.'*

I can still hear God's answer now, a conversation, in a gentle yet assertive tone as a father making a point to his daughter.

"Remember the dream I gave you before you had the girls?"

"Yes."

"Remember the day you prayed to be loved and I said, 'You will be friends first,' and that I was weaving your hearts together?"

"Yes, I remember, Lord."

"Remember I did not agree with the men coming into your life, and I did not approve your dating, because then you would have to explain yourself to them?"

"Yes I do, although I did not understand why."

"Remember I said that, although things will not be the way others will agree, I agree and I will be glorified. I told you I would remove him and strip him of all I have allowed him to obtain and the man worthy of you and your daughters will fill the shoes of father."

"Yes. I do! I do!"

Whimpering, I said, "You are a Good Father. You're my Daddy, God!"

What else was a girl to do at that moment but cry herself to sleep with hope in her heart and—oh yes—Steven now on her mind.

Daily I thanked Him so much for reminding me of my worth to Him and never forgetting about me or the dream . . . I know that, all along, His correction was Him loving me.

I was struggling alone so that He could be made strong in my weaknesses.

I was building my faith and character by refraining from any man who wasn't God's choice for me.

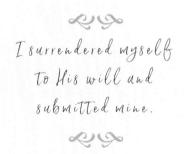

I surrendered myself to His will and submitted mine.

Oh how my love for my Daddy God, swelled in my heart. I surrendered myself to His will and submitted mine. To know that I was always on His mind felt complete; I felt whole; I felt important.

Love suffers long and is kind; love does not envy; love does not parade itself, is not puffed up; does not behave rudely, does not seek its own, is not provoked, thinks no evil; does not rejoice in iniquity, but rejoices in the truth; bears all things, believes all things, hopes all things, endures all things.

Love never fails. But whether there are prophecies, they will fail; whether there are tongues, they will cease; whether there is knowledge, it will vanish away.

ᔐ *1 Corinthians 13:4-8 NKJV*

I had my own personal experience of 1 Corinthians 13:4-8 and I was now convinced the man that He would bring would not complete me, but would be an extension of His love for me here on earth. Marriage is a life of giving and He gave me back everything that was taken from me in my first marriage. Every day I would ask God to take the fuzzy love at first sight feelings away for Steven. I did not want to awaken love before its time and he didn't feel the same. I could not explain why, the more I tried to get him off my mind, the worse it got. We were co-workers and we didn't mind being around each other.

Steven's girlfriend broke up with him and married three months later. As for my ex-husband, he never returned for a visit. Of course I called to find out his whereabouts, but he was nowhere to be found. Sadly he had gotten caught up in his messes and was serving time. I actually had an opportunity to reconcile with my ex-husband's parents later in life. My former mother-in-law shared that she prayed often for her son, and for her granddaughters, that they would grow up knowing God. I had closure on that side of the family, and my ex-husband remained with a life covered in prayer for when he was ready for his own breakthrough.

I enjoyed going to work for the first time ever! Boy was I smitten by those hellos and goodbyes from Steven. They were everything!

My confirmations…

While at work one day, since Steven and I had the same lunch hour, he asked if we could go to lunch together. I was screaming inside, "Yes!!!!" with a hallelujah choir playing in the background. I was on cloud nine until the time came for THE LUNCH. My nerves got the best of me. Although we did have casual talk from time to time, we had never sat across from each other face-to-face. WOW! He is even better looking than I thought. Butterflies were having a party. I could not look at him in the eyes. I felt the sweat bubbles on my upper lip and who could eat or sip water?

He began asking questions about my faith, so I shared my beliefs. He said he had been a devout Roman Catholic from the time of his upbringing. I knew he was because he would carry his bible in his backpack and would pray the rosary on his breaks. I 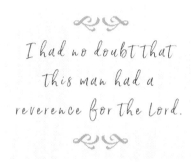 *I had no doubt that this man had a reverence for the Lord.* had no doubt that this man had a reverence for the Lord. Then the confirmation question came up. The very thing that Daddy God protected me and admonished me not to do, especially at work because of this question right here:

"Did you ever date anyone here at work?"

As if lightning had gone through my body. The Holy Spirit quickened me *'You hear that? Huh?'*

After my short pause and puzzled look I quickly said, "No." The heavens opened up that day and God had certainly worked to get this relationship to this point. Our friendship grew and now we were intentionally having lunch together. Phone conversations were daily. He was a family man who adored his mom, spoke highly of his dad, and the great relationships he had with both of his sisters. I can't forget to mention the attention he was giving me . . . priceless. He treated me like a lady and sincerely appreciated my company.

I still could not be around him without blushing, nor speak to him looking into his perfect brown eyes.

After months of friendship - nine to be exact - I received my second confirmation from Daddy God. "Remember I said You will begin as friends, for I have woven your hearts together."

'Oh man! Daddy you're the best but this is awkward. If I am hearing you correctly This man is THE MAN, but we are not even dating and he is not pursuing me.'

The longest silence was at that moment. He had never asked me out on dates because he knew my thoughts and feelings on dating. My girls come first and, if you wanted to see me outside of work, it's in a group and at my house. Unless he would commit to potentially wed, I was not going to cheapen my daughters' time away from me. He respected me and, after some time, he agreed we needed to give us a shot.

After a year of dating, my relationship with Daddy God took a back seat. Steven had all my attention and my daughters were getting used to seeing him. Every now and then, I would hear Daddy tell me "Julissa if you want 'marriage' you're going to have to let him go."

That was not You, Daddy. Impossible! The devil is a liar! This man is THE MAN.

Two years passed and Daddy God was not happy at all with our behavior. I had put Him up on shelf indulging in many late nights, sleepovers, partying, and clubbing. Though, what appeared natural felt so wrong. Convictions worsened and I needed to do something ASAP.

Three years in, we had a talk. I don't think any man, other than a God-fearing man, would respond the way he did. I told him the many times I had broken up with him were purely out of love and respect toward God, and not to do with my feelings toward him. I opened up my heart to him that he was still not ready for marriage, and for the first time, he understood, agreed, and was willing to end all those things that grieved the Holy Spirit.

That night I had a dream with me bathing a little boy while Steven recorded him. He had a big smile and big, beautiful, light brown eyes. I awoke and I heard clearly "his name is Nehemiah."

I never shared my dreams with anyone and I certainly was not going to tell this man, who was struggling with getting married, that I may very well be the mother of his son. I immediately went to the Bible to see if in fact this name was biblical and to find its meaning. I received the girls' names in a similar way, so I had to get confirmation. Nehemiah: "comforted by God" rebuilder of the Jerusalem walls. What a timely dream and perfect name. Unclear how it was going to unfold, I knew with certainty this was my husband and I, his wife. To the world, I would be obsessed, but to God, I was declaring and living from His promise.

Unfortunately, our agreement did not last long. How can we stop doing what we enjoyed doing together for five years?

Daddy God had ENOUGH! He said, "It ends now. Give him up! Give him back to me, like Abraham sacrificed Isaac. He is not ready for marriage and he won't be as long as your relationship continues this way."

Daddy God had ENOUGH!

"Wait what? You want me to let go of the man you say is my husband. I just invested five years, I'm head over heels in love with him, my girls adore him, and you want me to let him go? Daddy God, that is crazy. This is mind boggling."

I sobbed for days and breaking up was like pulling my heart out my chest. The pain was real. This was worse than my divorce. I truly didn't know nor could imagine life without him. Love certainly is patient and this is where I began to give what I so graciously received by Daddy God.

Three months of questioning, sleepless nights, crying, and screaming out of anger at myself. How could I allow myself to let it get this far. I would cry to work and cry myself back. At this point,

Steven had moved on to a new job. Everyone at work knew me as part of "us." Daily I would get asked how he was or how "we" were doing. Everywhere I went was a reminder of us, including the friendships we made together.

One day on my way home from work on the train with my shades on praying and crying, I poured myself out to Daddy God. I was tired of crying and feeling as if I lost. I was certainly convinced he was the man Daddy God had permitted in our lives. I was confused for a moment, questioning if I set myself up or was this really orchestrated by Daddy, Himself.

Then I heard, "Stop crying as if you're mourning the death of your relationship. It's not over. He will call you tonight."

I rushed home, got on my knees, and prayed. "I trust you, Daddy, and I know you won't hurt me, and I will never fail You."

He responded "You will fail, but I will be glorified."

Later that night, my phone rang, and it was Steven. He said, "Hello," and then hung up. It may not have been the call I anticipated, but it was enough to keep me going. This night changed my outlook on the days to come. Every reminder of him at work wasn't there to be rubbed in my face. Daddy purposely placed those people and things to keep me hopeful, and patiently waiting for the promise without fearing the future.

By the end of the third month, I was doing much better. Daddy God blessed me with two amazing women who stood by me and continually encouraged and lifted me in prayer. They supported my decision to obey and allow God to have His way. The more I prayed, the more I understood what Daddy was doing. Steven was battling his own commitment fears. His reality of being an instant dad to my girls made him uncertain, too. Since Daddy God is so awesome and perfect in all His ways, He needed to Steven to be certain of the woman he was set to marry, just as He needed to build patience in me.

One night, I was awakened by my phone.

Yes! It was him. Oh how I longed to hear his voice. I missed him so much. He went on by asking me to meet him by the train station down the block from me. By the sound of his voice, he had been drinking. He lived about two hours from me by train. I, being the woman of God that I promised to be, got a bottle of water and a puke bag, determined to send him on his way.

To my surprise he was waiting right outside my door. Those butterflies began to flutter, and for the first time I looked into his eyes and saw what Daddy had revealed; a broken man who truly loved me and was conflicted not in his love for me, but in himself. He hugged me tightly. The smell of alcohol was faint, so the smell of his cologne was everything. He began by telling me how he tried to, but couldn't look at women and compare them to me. He poured his heart out and cried. Surely as the Good Lord said, I failed. I was weak, and the one thing I swore I wouldn't do I did that night. I forfeited the wedding of my dreams for a night of pleasure.

Since I had to work later that morning, I got ready rather quickly and headed out. The guilt of conviction was immeasurable. I couldn't be happy, even if I tried. I disappointed Daddy God. How could I be happy that I got to see him. On the bus route, I sat in the back and cried hard; my soul begged for forgiveness and I heard Daddy gently say, "Yes. You have forfeited the wedding of your dreams and things will not be the same, nor easy, but I am the Lord your God and I keep my promises. I shall meet every need and tonight you have conceived. Remember your dream. His name is Nehemiah. Even in your weakness I will glorify Myself."

I was pregnant and I had no proof until weeks later. Steven was in disbelief and took time to understand. What he was fighting was what God had called him to be. In His mercy and grace, I gave birth to a healthy baby boy on 1/8/11. His name was a compromise at the time. Steven didn't understand how God could speak to me in dreams, so he had his doubts.

He said, "We should name him David – a man after God's own heart." This was the confirmation that removed all doubt.

I remembered praying for a King David. So, on that day, David Nehemiah Moreno was born. One year later, on the evening of a hot Memorial Day as the sun began to set outside, underneath the Verrazano bridge, Steven and I took our vows before Daddy God, our children, and our witnesses.

Some people may judge the route, but those are not people who know the mercy of the God of breakthroughs.

We have come a long way since then. Love is patient and a wise woman edifies her house. Shortly after our wedding, and to God be all the glory, my example of unshakeable faith and patience led Steven into a life of relationship with God. It was another dream manifested with lots more submission and self-dying that fulfilled another breakthrough in the Moreno household. Today, I can proudly say, "As for me and my household of Julissa, Steven, Sarah Elizabeth, Faith Ailynn, David Nehemiah, Isaac Elias, and Nathan Joseph, we will serve the Lord!

We certainly do not have a perfect love story, but it was definitely Daddy God-orchestrated. I am so glad He thought of me and my family before there ever was an "us." I am beyond blessed. He never changed His mind, despite my disobedience. He saw my heart. He saw my need. He waited on me. And He waited on the man He gave me for a husband.

Some people may judge the route, but those are not people who know the mercy of the God of breakthroughs.

JACQUELINE JASKE is a mother of two, a survivor, and an advocate. Writing her breakthrough story is a dream come true. It is written to empower others by sharing how her journey transformed from helplessness to hope. She is thankful every day for the blessings of God, family, and friends. Residing in Menomonee Falls, Wisconsin, she enjoys the lake, the outdoors, hiking, and kickboxing. Additionally, Jacqueline is a public speaker with the Wisconsin Department of Justice to help in the training of Initial Responders. You can learn more by contacting Jaqueline at **newendings11@gmail.com**. Jackie's son, Zack, whom you'll meet in her story, is today a compassionate First Responder working on his Bachelor of Science degree in Kinesiology and Doctor of Chiropractic, and - always - her gift.

Breakthrough

4

TAKE AWAY YESTERDAY

Jacqueline Jaske

When it's dark enough, you see the stars.

↳ Ralph Waldo Emerson

August 18, 1994...

I woke up alone in my bed, startled awake by the sound of voices coming from my living room. Subconsciously, I was wearing black to mourn the death within me. My sister, Sandi, had put me to sleep in the early morning hours, with my head on her lap as she ran her fingers through my hair like my Mom and Grandma used to do to comfort me when I was sick.

Tired.

Heartbroken.

I was all of those and more.

I returned to the scene . . . '*Why?*'

I needed something familiar, my feather pillow, my soft white bedding that used to bring me peace. I had to get to the living room to see if it was real, hoping it was all just a terrible nightmare. Too many thoughts were swirling around in my mind. My sisters were in the living room; they looked up at me with such pain in their eyes; it was all I needed to see to know it was real – it wasn't a nightmare.

I woke up to a reality that would change life as I knew it. I felt weak, nauseous, and numb. Grandma's blue chair, it was her favorite color, was waiting for me like her arms would be if she were still here. The tufted back and small arms of the chair embraced me as I curled up in her.

This death was so painful yet numbing. I was not angry; I was hurting – so deeply that it numbed every emotion, every bone, and every muscle. I felt lifeless. I didn't know what I was feeling, but somehow my body did. My eyes, like the crest of a waterfall, just poured. My tears were just there . . . a salty stream down my cheeks that just kept flowing.

My identical twin sister's eyes caught mine with sadness. The reflection in the mirror we shared showed me the depth of my own pain. I didn't want the pity that I would have from everybody knowing what just happened, yet I felt the pity for myself.

She reached out, touched my hand, and said, "What can I do?"

Looking out the window, the sun was shining so beautifully, as if nothing happened. I could feel its warmth through the window. The sky was a peaceful shade of blue, like an invitation. I still can't resist sunshine, I love the outdoors, the water, the heat . . . but I couldn't play that day. The world was just going on without me. I wanted to lasso the sun and pull it back in. I wanted the world to stop moving.

The cars were driving by, the clock was ticking, and I was halted . . . stopped dead in my tracks . . . frozen . . . paralyzed.

I didn't know how I would ever move again. How would I ever catch up with the world? What was I going to do?

I replied,

"YOU CAN TAKE AWAY YESTERDAY."

I was alive.

Zachary was alive.

We survived.

We were here to face it all.

I was not sure I wanted to be.

August 17, 1994...

I had an unusually early night and was excited to pick up my five-year-old son, Zachary, from the sitter. He would be starting Kindergarten in a week. Since I had been gone, we needed to go to the grocery store, with my little helper and maker of all things fun. My first born, my wish, my wouldn't-change-him-for-the-world little man. We will forever have this bond from our life-changing event.

He loved Pop-Tarts®, I'm pretty healthy but couldn't say no to his sweet face that night.

On the way out of the store it was so hot, we broke open the root beer popsicles and were having a ball, laughing, really being in the moment of being silly.

We drove home and unloaded the groceries. I gave Zachary his package of Pop-Tarts®, and he went to sit in my Grandma's blue chair in the living room. I walked through the narrow pantry hallway that led to the kitchen, the bright orange kitchen (I planned on painting). I opened the refrigerator door to my left, blocking the hallway from view. To my right was the back door with a deadbolt that required a key to open it from the inside; the key was missing. My back faced the sink.

As I was putting things in the fridge, that broken bottom shelf came loose again. I bent over trying to fix it when Zachary came and to my right side.

"Mommy can you help me open this?"

Yes; the Pop-Tarts®.

As I crouched down by my little man, I caught something out of the corner of my eye. A white shoe. *'Who does that shoe belong to?'* I turned and gasped quickly as a gloved hand covered my mouth and I felt the jagged blade of a knife at my throat. It happened in an instant.

'I can't breathe! I can't breathe! OH MY GOD WHAT IS HAPPENING, THIS CAN'T BE HAPPENING! SOMEBODY HELP! GOD PLEASE HELP!' I screamed in my head.

He led us to the dining room.

I grabbed the brown glove and moved his finger that was blocking my nose so I could breathe. Zachary let out a blood curdling terrifying scream like I had never heard before; no one else would hear it.

Our attacker yelled, "Do that again and I will kill your mother!"

Silent tears and screams I could only hear in my head, *'Someone help! PLEASE HELP!'*

We were standing in the dining room by the door to my bedroom, next to Grandma's bookcase. It was a beautiful, antique lawyer's bookcase with glass doors that lift up and inside. I was standing there and suddenly, in that moment, I felt a moment of peace in all chaos. There was a calm for just two seconds. In all this fear, for two seconds, I knew I wasn't going to die. I wasn't going to die and I was going to live through this.

Poof!

Gone!

Fear was back with a new dose of chaos and terror.

He took us into my bedroom and ordered Zachary to get on the bed. All I had was fear of, *'what is he going to do to my boy?!'*

'Don't let him see this!' I begged.

'What is he going to do to us!?' That question was so loud in my head! He had me against my wardrobe cabinet. I saw him for the first time. His wicked green eyes were piercing me through the nylon over his face; his nose and hair pressed flat, disguising this perverted monster.

He demanded that I take my underwear off and put on a pair of nylons he'd brought with him. Leaving my purple and black polka-dot skirt on, I did as he said and put on the cheap fabric with the cotton lining cut out. Humiliated and panic-stricken, my thoughts were on my son.

'*He can't see this!*'

I begged the attacker, "Please, don't let him see this!"

He took me out of the bedroom, back through the dining room, and to the bathroom behind the kitchen.

I was silently screaming to myself. '*God, what do I do?! THINK, THINK, THINK! Do I fight?! What do I do? Save your son!*'

'*Do what you have to do to survive*' is what I told myself. Period.

'*Live . . . so you can save Zachary!*'

First, he put me on the sink, lifted my skirt, and tried kissing me. I wouldn't give him my lips. He attempted to use every part of my body, but his own body wasn't working well enough, despite the times he painfully tried.

He ordered me down to the cold, black and white tiled floor – he was wearing a white shirt, very white, and red running shorts. His arms seemed weak, but his legs were muscular. '*He must be a runner.*' I didn't realize how important these observations would be until recounting them later.

He forced other unspeakable acts on me that don't deserve detailing. '*Do I punch him? Bite him? Just stay alive for Zachary! What if he stabs me and I can't save my boy? Do what you have to do to survive.*'

He asked me, "When will your husband be home?"

I quickly responded, "Any minute."

He didn't need to know I didn't have a husband. Could it be the ring I hadn't worn in years that I decided to put on that morning? It may have saved my life.

He seemed to panic as he ordered me, "Lay down on the floor and stay there!"

He grabbed the glass doorknob and stepped out of the bathroom. As I saw the door closing, I suddenly came alive again. It was a snap . . . like the flick of a switch . . . the pull of a lightbulb's string. I was a new superhero in complete contrast with the woman who died on the floor. I became empowered by a strength that wasn't my own. I realized I had to save my son. My actions, in a split second, became about Zachary and not me. Before the door closed, I grabbed the knob, not letting the terror of the possibility that he may be on the other side stop me. I had an adrenaline rush – the kind an accident witness experiences that allows him to lift away a whole car to save a life. I was electric in a moment. I couldn't let him take my son. I yanked the door open, fearless of where my attacker might be and knowing nothing would stop me from saving Zachary.

Taking back my power, I demanded, "STAY AWAY FROM MY SON!"

He had vanished. *'Is Zachary still here!?'* I ran to the bedroom in sheer terror, not knowing what I would find.

Safe on my bed, there sat my boy.

He looked so small surrounded by soft white bedding.

We were together.

We were alive.

We were together.

We were alive.

I don't remember if he walked out with me or I carried him out.

I grabbed the phone (the only one we had was in the dining room), locked the door, and called 911. Then, I called my sister, Sandi. I was hysterical as I told her I was raped, and I needed her. To this day, I cannot stand to hear or say that vulgar, violating four-letter-word.

She said, "I'm on my way!"

In a few minutes, I heard a loud bang on the door, and even though they announced themselves as the police I was terrified to open it. When I let them in, they asked if my attacker was still in the house. I hadn't thought of that. I didn't know.

Next, Sandi and her husband, my brother in law, Chad, were at the door. Sandi rushed in by Zachary sitting in the blue chair. I saw Chad standing in the doorway, and I was ready to fall into his welcoming hug. He was a safe protector.

The police stopped me. *'I need to be held. Why can't I be held?'* There might have been evidence on me. I needed to be held now more than any other time in my life. I felt nauseous, I was going to be sick. The smells, the tastes, the fear, and the panic swirled inside of me. I was spinning in the storm. I collapsed into my son's miniature recliner.

Sandi took Zachary to my older sister's house, just a couple miles away while I told the detectives the events of the night over and over and over and over and over again. All the while, Chad sat next to me on the floor holding my hand. He was such a loving support to me as I sat in Zachary's chair. I don't know why I sat in that tiny chair. Maybe because I felt so small, so empty.

Sandi came back to go with me to the hospital. On our way, I asked if Zachary had his Pop Tarts. Such a trivial thing to focus on, but they mattered. Those Pop Tarts were the last part of the life that was normal. She didn't see any; I had to know if he had them. In the early morning hours, Sandi returned home with me. My loving big sister; when I was a little girl she was the gentlest hair brusher, sliver puller, and bandage remover. Now, she sat in the bathroom with me where the death of my soul took place, while I tried to wash the humiliation from my body; a filth that wouldn't leave for years.

As I approach my bed, on auto-pilot...exhausted...in need of the escape only sleep or death can give me, at my feet on the floor, I find the Pop-Tarts®...still unopened.

Zachary and I had been pulled apart from each other. He was whisked away so quickly, with good intentions—to remove him from the turmoil and fear. But I needed to hold him. I needed to know he felt safe. *'Did I hug him in the moments following the attack?'* I didn't know. My baby boy must have been so afraid sitting by himself, not knowing what to do or what was happening, and I didn't even know if I held him! Twenty-four years later, on a night where the worst details are still clear, I remain foggy on this unanswered question. It still haunts me.

I needed to know he felt safe.

In the hours and the days that would follow, I would attend my funeral, only I was alive, kind of. I was a shell just observing everything going on. At first, I couldn't tell anyone but family, until it was publicly announced. It was an ongoing investigation and he was still on the loose.

People brought cards, flowers, food, teddy bears. Family and friends, old and new, came out of the woodwork to offer their condolences. This wasn't a celebration of life, it was the mourning of a death. What do you say to a living body that's dead inside? Their gifts were a memorial to the old me. I felt like I was out-of-body, observing these kindnesses, the phone calls, and messages of mourning. As with most grief, everybody wanted to be beyond it, but I was too numb in the immediate aftermath to absorb their comfort.

I had just moved into my lower-level flat three weeks earlier. How was I going to stay?

One of the best things someone said to me was, 'you didn't do anything wrong.'

I didn't do anything wrong.

I was in the wrong place at the wrong time and the wrong person happened to be there, too.

Detectives visited every other day. We moved to an upper flat.

I was called in to watch a videotape from the grocery store. He was there. He was watching us shop. I had no idea. He followed us home. A place a mother and child should feel safe, turned out to be the place he found us, and he was still out there.

'*Was he still watching us? Were we safe?*'

I was mad at God. I mean really angry!

'*Why? What did I do to deserve this? I am struggling as a single parent and now this?*'

As a child, and I guess as a young adult, I thought if I believed in God and was a good person I would be protected from evil.

My Christian friends told me about free will and bad things happening to good people because of it.

Their words were comforting in the moment, but I didn't get it.

Three weeks later…

I was invited to the "Beacon" support group; Sandi came with me. There I told my story to others who had similar experiences. They seemed shocked that I was there so soon. There were women here who this happened to three years ago, five years ago, eight years ago. When we left, I told Sandi I could not be in this place five years from now. My life could not be on hold for that long.

Two and a half months later…

He was caught. A bartender, twenty minutes north of where I lived, called the police from his suspicious behavior. They found the nylon mask, nylons, and a knife in his trunk, but it was a police officer across town, to the south, about forty minutes away from where he was caught, that thought it sounded familiar. He miraculously helped piece it together.

Then the court process started, and a promised ninety-day speedy trial was over a 390-day process.

Back to hell!

This was interrupting our life. Zachary's first day of school, the day before Thanksgiving, four days before Christmas, and many more "normal days" that were anything but normal. My life was like a TV with the judicial system holding the remote control.

ON.

OFF.

PAUSE.

REWIND. REPEAT. RELIVE.

Sitting on my couch at my new place, a stranger sitting with me told me what my attacker said in his pre-sentencing interview.

She looked at me, maybe immune to this or hardened by it, and said, "He intended to kill you. Did you know that?"

"No, and I don't think I need to know it now."

Then, I remembered that moment of unexplained peace, knowing for certain I would live. '*How could that be when she just told me he planned on killing me? Then why did I live?*' Reality was taking hold of me, I was not supposed to be here right now; I was supposed to be dead. '*I am alive. There must be a reason; a purpose. What is my purpose?*' Little did I know I would spend the next 24 years stumbling into it.

November 17, 1995...

The week before Thanksgiving, he was sentenced to the stiffest sentence in the state of Wisconsin; 115 years with the recommendation that his first parole in 2024 be denied.

This was my focus for so long; I really didn't know how to function without the goal in front of me of putting him behind bars for the rest of his life—so I could get on with mine.

Over the next few years I fell flat on my face . . . not living the celebration of my life.

Was this on purpose or was it my punishment? It felt like a punishment at the moment, the hell I was living in. I could live in moments, I could work, but—at the end of the day when sun started to go down—the fear would come back. I fought closing my eyes every night. I slept on the couch with the lights on and rarely slept through the night. In my nightmares, we hid and planned our escape, over and over, different scenarios. In my nightmares, like that night, I couldn't scream.

August 17, 1997...

On a camping trip, someone who didn't know my story was waiting for me to walk down the trail in the dark. They jumped out from behind a tree with a flashlight shining up at their faces. I SCREAMED! I couldn't breathe, I couldn't speak, I was paralyzed with fear . . . but I screamed a blood curdling, like-I-was-stabbed, scream.

Hypnotherapy was recommended. It was never meant to hurt me, but it was a terrifying way to relive my experience and brought very vivid nightmares with it.

Actually sleeping . . . this didn't happen often and, when it did, it was not for very long.

The man who destroyed my life as I knew it entered my peaceful sleep. This time it was different; he knew I saw him. He started chasing me with a very large knife, much larger than the actual knife used that night. I was running up a spiral staircase made of stone and the walls were cold and damp. It resembled a castle tower where a princess is held captive until she is rescued. I was imprisoned in my life. I was held captive by my rapist who held my life until I chose to take it back.

The tables turned; I was chasing him. I caught him, and he fell to the cold stone floor. I forcefully and viciously stabbed him over and over and over. With each thrust of the knife, I felt vindication; for traumatizing my son! For terrifying us! For taking away our sense of security! For the tears! For the fear! DIE! He doesn't bleed and he won't die! Why won't he die!? DIE! DIE! DIE! YOU DESERVE TO DIE!

I brought this invaded dream to my therapist, and as I started to relive it, this is what I learned:

I was being held captive in the tower, a prince was not going to rescue me. (I had to admit I would really like the prince part of the story). I was held captive by my inability to move forward in my life without letting go of the past. And the role reversal . . . I think trying to kill him was for all the fight in me I couldn't let out that night. It was quite cathartic even if it was my subconscious that let it out. He wouldn't or couldn't die because he was alive, and the death was in me. This was a breakthrough and a relief to know I understood one piece of what was going on within me . . . one step at a time.

Five Years Later...

In August of 1999, I was called by the Beacons group to write a paragraph about my experience five years earlier. It started, "The next morning I subconsciously wore black...."

After the meeting, I had reached my goal from five years ago that I truly was no longer in that place. I was no longer a victim; I was a survivor. I would never forget and there were trigger moments, nightmares, and days of despair, but I was learning to move forward.

Seven Years Later...

We were back in court.

His parents wanted to move back to Croatia and wanted him deported to serve the rest of his sentence there.

'WHAT!?"

"How is this happening?'

Okay, I'd had it.

August 17, 2001...

I received a phone call—the heavy accent and the words revealed his identity.

"I wish you were dead," he said.

Panic took over! 'Is he in my house!? Is he watching me and my family!?' I contacted the police in our new community and shared why this was not just a prank call.

Upsetting my world again!? I don't think so!

I was not going to be silent anymore. I called the media and was interviewed. I'm not sure if that did anything, but it made me feel better for speaking out and the parents' plea was thrown out of court.

Eleven Years Later...

By accident on purpose, meaning purely my accident but God's purpose, I found a book on the booth seat of a café I visited frequently. It had a note on the front that boldly stated:

PLEASE READ ME.

That's how *The Shack,* by William P. Young, came to me. In it, an act of violence takes a child from her family. I cried my way through it.

What changed my direction in life was the main character asking, "God where were you?"

God's reply? "I was there the whole time."

It hit me over the head, slapped me in the face, and embraced me. God *was* there the entire time. I was supposed to die that night. I didn't. I must still have a purpose here on earth. I believe God whispered to me that morning, "Wear the ring."

He was there alongside me. It was the start of my journey with Him . . . *the most valuable breakthrough.* He saved us that night and He used this tragedy to lead me onto the path of my faith walk with Him.

Faith is taking the first step when you don't see the whole staircase.

Martin Luther King Jr.

I now realize that the reason I couldn't see the whole staircase was because I am supposed to build it. I had been so busy trying to build it without the right tools. I finally understood, GOD IS MY TOOLBOX, to repair, replace, or patch the broken boards of my staircase one step at a time.

He was there, He is here, and He always will be.

I was mourning the loss of who I thought I was meant to be, instead of building toward my new purpose in a saved life.

Becoming a survivor is a process. Building and climbing one stair-at-a-time. There will be struggles and PTSD, but there will also be joys and celebrations and accomplishments.

Becoming a survivor is a process.

I celebrate honoring my own worth. My desire for strength and joy has grown larger than my fear. I have learned to replace fear with trust.

"Fear, you will never be welcome here!"

❧ *Francesca Batistelli*

I recognize with gratitude, the struggles God has placed before me that have led me up the staircase, *closer to Him*. Finding the strength in the struggle of each step with my Toolbox by my side for the climb. Through God's grace, I understand that who I am meant to be is who I have become.

YESTERDAY IS GONE!

In peace I will lie down and sleep, for you alone, Lord, make me dwell in safety.

❧ *Psalm 4:8*

MEET YOUR BREAKTHROUGH AUTHOR

AMY SIKKEMA is a widow and mom of two busy boys and one spunky little girl. Grand Rapids Michigan is where she resides and eagerly serves Jesus. Her passion for reaching out to the lost and hurting has led her to her calling. Writing, blogging, and speaking the good news of hope and God's promises are her mission. Amy serves on the board of the no-profit organization *"Shields of Hope- West Michigan"* where she walks alongside families who are battling cancer. In her down time Amy enjoys camping, sunsets over Lake Michigan, and gathering friends and family around bonfires in her backyard. You can follow Amy at **amysikkema.com** or on Facebook- search **Sikkemastrong**.

Breakthrough

5

IT'S OKAY, YOU DIDN'T KNOW

Amy Sikkema

It's okay; you didn't know. You were just a dreamer, girl. You twirled your skirt so pretty. You played for hours building forts in the woods. You were always the princess with Prince Charming and three little kids. You were pretending to have it all.

It's okay; you didn't know. You were so timid inside. You were trying to hide the pain behind the big smile – trying to find where you fit in - conforming to what others might accept instead of letting it go.

It's okay; you didn't know. You were free . . . independent. You had the whole world at your fingertips. You were hungry to grow and wanted success. You worked hard and played harder. You had goals. You had plans. They were perfect and so was life.

It's okay; you didn't know. He was tall and made you laugh. He was who you dreamt of when you slept and the first thing you thought of when you woke up. He took your insecurities and threw them across the ocean. He was your prince.

It's okay; you didn't know. You experienced the greatest joy of having your newborn baby boy to hold in your arms after not meeting the one who came before him. He would change everything, from how you saw the world, to how the world stared right back at you. How the days can go so slowly, and years so fast. You were both new parents. You didn't know, but you were ready to tackle it together.

It's okay, you didn't know your family wouldn't grow as quickly as you hoped. You asked why. You waited and prayed. There were tests and drugs. After many years, and thousands of tears, miracle number two.

It's okay; you didn't know. It was stressful. Life was busy. Headaches were more constant. You saw the changes, but thought everyone goes through this. You'll get through it. You always did.

It's okay; you didn't know. You leaned over and whispered, "surprise, number three!" and saw pure joy, and shock on his face.

It's okay; you didn't know he had a massive brain tumor.

It's okay; you didn't know. You had no clue how a community would rally around your family. You didn't know you'd pour your entire existence into saving his life, though it continued to slowly, yet so ever-so-quickly slip away. You gave all of yours to save his.

It's okay; you didn't know how crushing it would be to tell him it's okay to go home.

"Go be with Jesus."

It's okay; you didn't know the only isle your daughter would be walking down with her daddy would be behind his casket, not on his arm. The pain, and howl from your oldest sons' lips would mimic the cry of your own tender heart.

It's okay; you didn't know what to do.

It's okay; you didn't know some would walk away when they promised to stay.

It's okay; you didn't know how strong you were.

It's okay; you didn't know. You didn't know how, all along, He was shaping you. You didn't know how He was going to use you. You didn't know how He was preparing you.

It's okay; you didn't know how much He loves you – how much He cares for you – how much He longs for you. He even died for you.

You don't know the great plans He has for you – how He's going to prosper you – the bright future He has for you.

It's okay; you didn't know . . . He had to break you to remake you.

Have you ever experienced a time when you were suddenly questioning everything about, well, everything? *What is this all worth? What is the purpose? Why?* Quite mundane questions in a world that would have you settle for *less-than* the prosperous life of God. The thing is, God is anything but mundane and wants anything but *less-than* for us. He wants us to be spirit-filled truth seekers . . . life speakers to our world that is filled with darkness and hurt. His desire is for us to thrive, not strive. He longs for us to be made whole through Him and nothing else. When we whole heartedly give our every beautiful and broken piece to Him, He will take it, mold it, and break through every chain surrounding it. This breaking of chains will cause a ripple effect, a *Breakthrough Effect.*

God is anything but mundane.

I was blessed to grow up just outside of the beautiful city of Grand Rapids in a quiet suburb on the country outskirts of West Michigan. My parents divorced when I was ten-years old and I resided with my mom full-time, visiting my dad on Tuesday nights and every other weekend. My mom, a strong faith-based and God-fearing woman, prayed for us every single night. We attended church every Sunday in the morning and evening, in addition to Wednesday evening. Mom made sure we were fed scripture and life.

I am also the eldest of four girls. Growing up, we always had someone to talk with, fight with, and "borrow" clothes from.

I cut my Barbie™ doll's hair in my constant mercy with new, "trendy," short hairstyles. And that, my friends, is where my hairdressing career began. Entering high school, my love for the hair industry and the creative outlet it provided became my drive. I graduated from high school and hair school and so it all goes – MY plans were coming together perfectly.

It all looked lovely: those five-, ten-, and twenty-year plans.

To my surprise, while in my senior year, I had also met the man that God reserved for me. A tall, blonde, Dutch boy with a most caring, mischievous smile . . . a smile that would rescue him from any impending predicament. He was a good man and a bad boy; *the* lethal combination. He also had a big ol' pickup truck. And well, you know, Joe Diffie said it best: "There's just something 'bout a pickup man!"

He was a good man and a bad boy.

Our meeting of the hearts came a little early for us to marry, according to *our* plan – the plan that states you must have all your ducks in a row. So, we got our ducks in a row and five years later we tied the knot.

Life was good, repetitive, comfortable, safe, and fun. Kevin worked at a local greenhouse year-round and had just joined the local fire department. Most days, he would waltz through the door smelling of dirt, sweat, and coffee. From time to time, the scent from working a structure fire would waft from his clothes. I found myself often routinely scolding him for putting his dirty hands on the white trim of the front door to hold his balance while he slipped off his work boots.

"Did you even wash your hands today?" I would ask in disgust.

"Yes, dear. It's just imbedded in my skin, 'cause I'm a hard-working man!" he would reply.

He would then proceed to chase me around the kitchen with his big smile and playful kisses.

It was wonderful.

I would later long for those dirt marks on the white trim.

I worked full time at a local high-end hair salon. The challenges faced were many, and it became my custom to meet them with an "I'm in total control" attitude. I quickly realized it was a job that required a lot of patience and self-sacrificial service. There were days with no lunch because "Betty" wanted extra highlights. She just found out she has stage 3 breast cancer and will lose her hair soon. Or "Missy's" mom died yesterday, so squeezing her in and staying two hours past closing time was never a second thought. These stories stirred the pot in my soul. It was a pot that wanted more. It wanted to pour out more Christ-like love. It began wanting less control and desired less perfection.

For a year, Kevin and I played the newlywed game and, I must say, we did it very well. The only hardships we allowed to face us would be choking down a few of my home-cooked (burnt) meals and the big decision of which couples we would want to schedule out our weekends with. *Oh those days . . . blissful, yet blind . . . mainly at what was to come.*

After several months of honing my cooking skills so they were acceptable enough to feed a child and praying about the best time, we decided it was a good time to grow our little family. Struggling with an endometriosis diagnosis at a young age, the reality of an easy-to-conceive pregnancy was put on the back burner. My mantra was: hope for the best – plan for the worst.

A few short weeks later, much to our surprise, two blue lines! Everything was running smoothly and right on schedule with our plan. Until . . . it wasn't. Three weeks later, I miscarried our first baby.

That moment was a taste of grief and the shocking, shaking reality of how little control we have in our lives. God showed up and poured out His compassion, His mercy and love He has for the grieving heart. Though we never held our first baby in our hands, I do believe that child is now in Heaven; waiting on a reunion that is very much anticipated on this side of eternity as well.

The seasons changed from winter to spring to summer to fall. Following the season of pain from the miscarriage and healing, we were blessed to have two blue lines again. Nine months later, a healthy baby boy. And that is when *it* really began. The it? A big tug at my heart. There is something more. There will be something more. Prepare yourself for more. I began to get into prayer on a very regular basis. I prayed for clarity, strength, and discernment, for guidance and wisdom, and for peace. Yet, my soul was far from peace.

EARTHQUAKE
"Give me your eyes, Lord!
So, I can see who needs to see you"
The price is high, my child.
"Give me your love
for the ones who feel forgotten or left behind!"
The price is high.
"Give me your heart
for those whose hearts are breaking!"
The price is high, princess...
How far will you go, chosen one?
"I will go anywhere"
What will you do with this?
"I will do as you call"
What will you lay down?
"It all"
"The price would be too high not to.
YOUR PRICE, Lord, was enough."

Years after our eldest son was born, having a second baby was proving to be a more difficult and time-consuming journey. Months without a second baby in my arms turned into years and my heart began to grow weary.

'Why isn't our plan happening? We are good people who love God and we know that God wants to bless His people with a full quiver. So, what gives?'

In our own subtle way, we began to question God's will and plan. (A word of advice: try not to question God's will and plan.) Our God is bigger and better than we can ever imagine and He sees and knows things we cannot possibly fathom.

This questioning left me far more restless and discontent than ever before. We decided to start a journey with fertility. The years of treatments, hormones, pokes, prods, and doctors' appointments began to take its toll both emotionally and physically. Month after month of negative tests were exhausting our hope to expand our family. Rest was what I needed, so rest was what we did.

Taking a few years off from fertility treatments proved to be an incredible time of growth and reflection. We prayed, and focused our energy on another avenue of expanding our family we felt God may have been calling us to: foster care and adoption with special consideration of refuge fostering. We went to a meeting at a local agency to learn more about the commitment of what that responsibility entailed. Leaving the meeting, my husband and I decided to take time and pray about the choice and, after time and reflection, we felt God was encouraging us to lay the fostering option aside – at least for that time being.

A few short days after deciding not to foster, the massive earthquake of 2010 hit Haiti. I remember walking into the local gym that afternoon. It was warm and you could hear the buzzing of the fans all around. The smell of rubber and sweat hit all at once when opening the doors. I headed to the treadmill and the images flashing on the screen above broke me.

'All those people, all of that devastation. They already have so little and now they have nothing.'

I wanted to do something. I needed to do something. The pot in my soul was bubbling. My heart cried out for them.

Coming home that afternoon from the gym with those images fresh on my mind, I poured my heart out to my husband. He sat in our kitchen and listened to each hurting word I spoke.

"I fully and totally support you in whatever God is calling you to do, "he told me. The thing was, I had no idea what exactly he *was* calling us to as my heart was breaking. I prayed and cried out to God in that moment, begging him to give me deep purpose for this broken heart. This broken heart that would soon break even deeper, spilling out all of what was held in that pot deep in my soul.

Miracle babies...

Every trial that we pass through is capable of being the seed of noble character. Every temptation that we meet in the path of life is another chance of filling our souls with the power of heaven.

⤳ *Frederick Temple*

After our respite from fertility treatments, we decided to give **it** one last try. We prayed boldly for a child. God, in all His goodness, and in His perfect timing, answered our prayer. We praised God for the gift of our fiery, red-headed second son who was born after five years of questions, grief, and heartache. We believed our family was complete.

God had other plans. He was breaking chains.

Shortly after our fertility baby turned one, much to our surprise, two blue lines. A third baby. A miracle baby.

The same time the blue lines appeared, so did headaches for my husband. Once a month to once a week. Then came the loss of peripheral vison and a numb leg. I knew deep down that something was *not* okay. After arguing to get him to go in, I called the doctor and explained, in grave detail, his symptoms.

"If he has another headache before this appointment we schedule, he will have to go to the ER and be seen."

Two days later, he had another.

Walking into the lobby of the Emergency Room, all I could see were the beige walls and black runner carpets stretched under my feet. I held my five-month pregnant belly, quietly whispering "it's going to be okay," as we followed the nurse to the exam room. The entire walk, I was thinking about our boys and our miracle baby, and begging God for another miracle in that room.

After a neuro exam and assessment of his symptoms, the doctor told us that he believed Kevin was suffering from complicated migraines, but to be on the safe side, he ordered a CT scan.

As the wheels on the hospital bed squeaked their way down the hallway, I sat in anticipation of what was next. Every second on the clock seeming like ages. Revealing memories of our love, and thoughts of our hopes and dreams were ticking by.

Five minutes later, the doctor sheepishly opened the heavy exam room door, quietly closed it behind him, and sat down next to me.

I knew something was wrong.

He told me the CT scan revealed a large mass on his brain and he would have to be transported to another hospital immediately for further testing. An ambulance arrived shortly after seeing the doctor, and brought my husband to the large hospital downtown.

I knew something was wrong

The next day, the softball-sized brain tumor was removed. Pathology came back and revealed it to be a Glioblastoma, the most aggressive and deadly form of brain cancer.

We wept . . . I imagine the type of weeping that Jesus did.

To say our lives were thrown upside down would be an understatement. From prenatal appointments and well child visits, to chemo and radiation. Witnessing the toughest, strongest, bravest man I had ever known be physically crippled by seizures due to a brain tumor was devastating. He was overwhelmed by the nausea and exhaustion from chemo.

And then came our baby girl – a surprise ray of hope during the storm – a true gift and blessing from God himself. She was beautiful in every way. I found myself in awe of how beautiful our boys were, how beautiful our love was, and how much peace we were receiving during this time. Peace for which the only explanation is that it was given from the Prince of Peace Himself, our Heavenly Father. Our faith was in the fire. Being refined, our eyes opened to the ones who were far from our reach before. We clung to His Hord and His promises and He never failed and never gave up on us.

Count it all joy when you fall into various trials, knowing that the testing of your faith produces patience.

James 1:2-3

During the cancer battle and his last days, our faith significantly shifted. We let go of all control, all desire for our own plan, and said, "Here we are, Lord. Send us."

A week later, Kevin was called home and received his healing. We rejoiced that his physical body was no longer in pain and struggling. Grief took over the landscape and backdrop of our children's and my lives.

I felt completely out of control and broken. The life we knew and built together was shattered. The pain was crushing. The boiling pot that was stirring in my soul began spilling over in every area of my life. I could not fix any of it. Not a single piece. So, I gave it to God. What he did and is doing is extortionary.

These trials will show that your faith is genuine. It is being tested as fire tests and purifies gold- though your faith is far more precious than gold. So when your faith remains strong in many trials, it will bring you much praise and glory and honor on the day when Jesus Christ is revealed to the whole world.

꙳ *1 Peter 1:7*

Knowing that I would see my husband again gave me hope. The eternal hope we have in Jesus is what pulled me through the sludge of grief on many dark days. Trying to find a "new normal" in a world that looked anything but normal was excruciating. Yet, there it was. Again and again. Peace that passed all understanding showed up at the most crucial of times. I had the divine reassurance that all of this was not in vain and that God would bring beauty from the ashes.

In my moments of surrender, even during our cancer journey, I began to write. It became my outlet for my emotions. It was a way for me to share what God was speaking to my heart and mind without my voice getting in the way. I would write for hours for myself, and share publicly our grief as well. I felt God was leading my hands to write our cancer journey. So I did. Reliving many of the early moments were healing and breaking all over again. There were points in our journey that I continuously became "stuck" on and I'd begin to grieve it again.

Two years into writing the unfinished memoir, I felt God's call to grief writing. It felt as though I needed to set the cancer story aside, dive into grief, and write it all out. It's as though God had chains he wanted to break.

"Grief devotional, grief devotional," he continued to speak to my heart. It left me a bit confused on how to move forward.

"Lord, You are all-knowing, but this I do not know. I do not know Your plan. I do know You are good. Through You we have bright hope and a future. I know You will prosper us, but I do not know what this means or how I will do this."

For months, I prayed on what God wanted me to write as I continued to grieve and move forward.

Enter my friend, Kimberly, who happened to own a Christian publishing company.

For quite some time I had found myself with a note pad by my side to jot down anything and everything that came to my mind or heart. During my first conversation with my friend, it was no different. She reached out to me on a beautiful March evening and we chatted about life and briefly shared what each other had endured. As we were talking, the words "Philippians 4:12" kept coming to my mind.

Not thinking too much on it, but curious of what the scripture was, I wrote it down.

At the end of our conversation, I was invited to write in two books . . . one being a grief devotional. *'Wow God!'*

He sure has an amazing way of having all the details in place. Sometimes we get so caught up in our own ways and striving that we don't allow Him to do what He does best: have control and be God. We need to allow Him to break through and show us His mighty power.

I arrived home that evening, excited and eager for what God was putting in motion. I sat down at my kitchen table and opened my Bible, anticipating what I would read when I opened to that scripture in Philippians. Flipping the pages faster and faster, I knew that God was about to reveal something to me and I couldn't wait to see what.

> *I know what it is to be in need, and I know what it is to have plenty. I have learned the secret in being content in every situation, whether well fed or hungry, whether living in plenty or in want.*
> *Philippians 4:12*

My jaw dropped as I continued to read on.

> *I can do all things through Christ who gives me strength.*
> *Philippians 4:13*

When my husband was finished with his first round of chemo and radiation treatments, he and his siblings and I decided to get tattoos to permanently signify our support for him. When I sat in the parlor chair and had the artist sketch, this was the only symbolism that repetitively came to my mind.

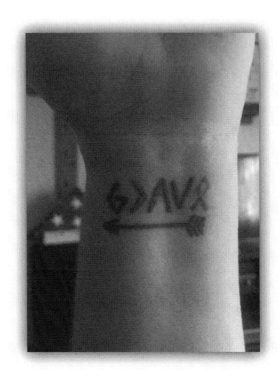

God (**G**) is Greater than (**<**) the highs (**^**) and lows (**v**), combined with the **brain cancer ribbon** (which was a Philippians 4:12 experience) and an **arrow** pointing to Christ (which is a Philippians 4:13 promise). And, together, the symbols help me remember that Christ walked out of the **GRAVE**, overcoming death, itself.

These symbols mean so much more to me now, three years after the loss of my husband. I have God's affirmation and love upon it directly from scripture.

I could hardly believe what I was reading. I know how good a Father He is. He chose to speak directly to me and in a very personal place, affirming that this was exactly where He wanted me.

He had to break me. Maybe He must break you or let you become broken to remake you. In that breaking, He will refine, polish, and prepare. He breaks the chains.

His praise will ever be on my lips.

Truth

You need two kinds of truth to break through. I call them "Big T Truth" and "small t truth."

"BIG T TRUTH" is not a thing, it's actually a Person. You must know the Person of Jesus Christ, who is *"the Way, the Truth, and the Life."* (John 14:6) "Big T Truth" is also The Word of God. John told us that Jesus was the *"word made flesh, who dwelt among us."* (John 1:14) That means Jesus and The Word are Truth. And Truth is transformative! The Love of Jesus and The Word of God change us from the inside out! (And let's be honest, most of the time, the breakthroughs we need are an inside job!)

I like to think of "SMALL T TRUTH" as a reality check. I guess because that is one of the things that set me free in the biggest way! To get my breakthrough, I had to face the hard, ugly truth about myself, my loved ones, and my life. "Small t truth" flies in the face of denial. It brings real things—scary things, out of hiding. In my life, it sounded something like this:

He is an addict and he is not getting better.

This is not love, it's abuse.

Knowing Jesus and The Word of God leads us to breakthroughs when paired with facing the hard small t truths in our lives.

"....you will know the truth, and the truth will set you free."

John 8:32

DANELLE SKINNER loves her family tremendously. They inspire her to become her best. She says, "I am very much a work-in-progress." She studies Jesus and His ways in the Bible to become kinder, more patient, and more love-focused. It is there Jesus helps her on her journey to become a better version of herself. Changing her little by little from the inside out. She wants to encourage you to dig into His word, unpacking what it means for your life today, not just for eternity in Heaven. It will put life into your mind, body and soul. Glory to Him! Find Danelle on Facebook and reach her by email at: *SayYesToThe Journey@gmail.com.*

Breakthrough

6

IDENTITY CRISIS IN CHRIST

Danelle Skinner

 elf-Identity refers to the global understanding a person has of themselves.

identity

[ī'**den**(t)ədē]

noun

1. *the fact of being who or what a person or thing is*

Identity is composed of relatively permanent self-assessments, such as personality attributes, knowledge of one's skills and abilities, one's occupation and hobbies, and awareness of one's physical attributes. Have you ever wondered, *'who am I?'* For me it seems I experience identity loss every time my worldly identity changes. In

2013, I had to make the decision to end my Pediatric Hematology, Oncology, and Bone Marrow Transplant Nurse career for health reasons. I became a stay-at-home mom and that change took me on a roller coaster ride of emotions. It almost completely wrecked me. That's the thing about worldly identities. They are often rooted in the past. People tend to identify with who they *have been*, not with the potential of who they *can become*.

I wondered, '*Who am I? Who am I, without my fancy job title? How did I get here? How could I disappear? This is not what I thought my identity would be?*'

I was so good at being a nurse; it came naturally. I realize now, God had given me tools to ease the sheer panic parents felt when their world's as they knew it came crashing down with a child's cancer diagnosis. For that reason, I was often given the newly diagnosed families. It was a physically demanding and heart-wrenching, but I loved the beauty that shone through tragedy and now know God had equip me for that role.

It was physically demanding and heart-wrenching, but I love the beauty that shone through tragedy.

I was able to use the gifts he gave me, to guide parents, mainly the moms. He gave me a heart for moms even before I was one! I held them up spiritually and sometimes even physically, when they could barely stand and until they could stand on their own again. I achieved, thrived, and advanced quickly in that role. People saw me there, they knew me; my peers trusted me and knew they could count on me. They even gave me words and awards of affirmation. I found an identity and worth there!

The transition to staying at home was difficult for me. I had zero control over my spouse or my kids. I couldn't keep them from doing and saying and reacting however they were going to. I couldn't even fire them if they acted inappropriately or if they completely wrecked the work I just finished. I tried explaining to my husband, it's like mini failure after mini failure all day long. I'd give someone a bath, then they'd get dirty. I'd change a diaper, then they'd poop. I'd get everything ready to go, put them in their car seats then someone would say, "I need to go potty," and don't even get me started on "booty calls!"

"Mom, I'm done, can you wipe me?"

WHEN just WHEN will they wipe their own butts and WHEN will they just leave me alone while I wipe mine? I have a vision of ten tiny fingers reaching under the door crying for mommy, as I shut the door to have a silent, painful, helpless cry.

I'd tell them not to hit, they'd turn around and hit.

Don't touch that, so they'd touch it.

I'd clean something and then they would make another mess.

There'd be a dump truck worth to sweep every time I feed them which seemed to be six plus times a day. Toddlers are like little tornados. They certainly know how to make a mess in record breaking time. I've heard it said that trying to keep a house clean with toddlers is like trying to brush your teeth while eating Oreos!

As a nurse, I was a success; as a mom I was . . . well, I didn't know *who* I was and that was the real problem. Tell me this; when you first meet someone new. What is their first question? *"So, what do you do for a living?"*

I didn't know who I was and that was the real problem.

When you are not confident in your decision to stay home, their replies can be damaging. *"Oh, good for you, that must be nice."*

As if to imply you must sit at home doing nothing all day! Little did they know, it would have been the easy way out for me to go back to work because nursing came more naturally to me than being a homemaker. I found myself spending each day doing everything in my power to try to make sure my husband and kids were thriving in every possible way. I was finding myself, just trying to survive the day. Motherhood is a world of few, if any, words of affirmation. No awards. No advancing in this new role. I felt there was no room for an identity for me. Only my husband's, the kid's, and even the house's. After I was finished tending to all their identities, wants and needs, I didn't have enough energy left to tend to mine. So, I put me last. I completely lost myself, my identity, and my self-worth.

My husband and I have separate walk-in closets. I thank the Lord for that! Please tell me you have a secret place like this in your home? A place where everything you don't have the time or energy for gets thrown for another day? After I cleaned our house and put everyone's laundry away, I would come to my stuff and my laundry last. It wasn't just my physical laundry that I stuffed away. I also put away my "dirty laundry," the things I wasn't ready to handle. I wasn't dealing with the fact that I did not have measurable success as a parent. I wasn't pouring into my marriage. I wasn't building my relationship with God. I'd check in with myself. 'Do you have the energy to care for this stuff? To put it away?'

Often, I did not, so I'd throw it in the closet, shut the door, and fall into bed. Nothing left.

There is a reason flight attendants tell us, "In case of an emergency, place your oxygen mask on yourself before helping your kids."

'Hello!' If we don't have oxygen, we will pass out and, if we pass out, we are no good to our kids. This is the same with motherhood. If mothers have not taken care of themselves, they have nothing of value to give their husband, their kids, or others!

I was struggling. I was broken, depressed, and anxious. Did anyone see me? Know me? Love me without conditions? Who was I? What was I living for? What legacy would be told of me?

At the time, I did not know about Satan's plan against us to steal, kill and destroy. I realize now he was targeting me, my family, and my life! If the Lord hadn't pulled me gently to His Word, Satan would have succeeded! He had stolen my joy! He had killed my identity in Christ. He had buried it. I didn't even know it existed and all I could hear was Satan's voice whispering, "You are NOT enough."

To top it off, he was slowly destroying my family. He had us convinced our spouse was our enemy. As you can imagine, with no joy, no identity, and being married to my "enemy," all I felt was emotional, spiritual, and physical pain. I was drowning in self-pity and self-hate.

I felt I was failing and I wondered, *'Did I marry into slavery as a homemaker?'*

My opinion didn't matter, my needs always came second to others (at best). I literally lost my ability to laugh. I felt zero joy and it was physically and emotionally painful to fake a smile. The weight of the world was on my shoulders.

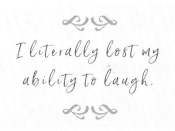

I literally lost my ability to laugh.

It turned out that identity loss wasn't the only thing pushing me down. Postpartum depression, physical illness, and the devil whispering "you aren't good enough," added to the weight.

As I recall that time in my life, I can't help to think of Moses. I cannot carry all these people by myself; the burden is too heavy for me. (Numbers 11:4) Moses must have physically felt the weight pressing down on him, like I did. He carried all God's people on the journey to the Promised Land. I was only carrying myself, my husband, and my kids. Moses must have been a physically, spiritually, and emotionally strong man!

My house felt heavy. It felt lonely. It felt like work. It felt like it pointed its finger at me with condemnation and judgement.

I remember telling my counselor, "For some reason I've been having a hard time breathing, I been noticing I hold my breath often!"

"Sometimes, holding your breath is a protection mechanism," she told me.

What was I protecting myself from? Was I protecting myself from what I thought my life would be like and feel like, but wasn't?

Protecting myself from the thought that being a stay-at-home Mom was too hard for me? Or the thought that to me doing laundry, dishes, cooking, cleaning, toddler fight mediation, and wiping butts all the time was completely mundane to me? That the amount of screaming and crying and demanding was maddening? Protecting myself from the fact that the anxiety, heaviness, and depression was close to drowning me? Was I protecting myself from my new consciousness that I didn't even know who I was or what my purpose was? Or was I protecting myself from the awareness that I was empty, thirsty, and longing for something else, anything else?

My counselor replied, "Let me ask you this, do you know your identity in Christ?"

No, I had no idea what he meant. My identity in Christ? Why do I not know? I knew *about* Jesus, but I did not know Him. I had never read the Bible to learn His heart and His character and I certainly didn't have a "relationship" with Him. I realized later, the weight of the world on my shoulders was the weight of who I thought I was supposed to be and who the world was telling me my identity had to be . . . all the things I wasn't.

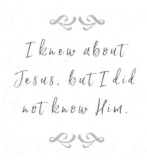

I knew about Jesus, but I did not know Him.

I'm thankful I physically felt the weight pushing me down. It was notification to me that something must change! It gave me a reason to fight for myself – to search for my identity in Him, my worth, and the true meaning of me. I had no idea where to start, but as soon as that desire to help myself was born, I heard God knocking.

> *Behold, I stand at the door and knock. If anyone hears my voice and opens the door, I will come in to him and eat with him, and he with me.*
>
> *Revelation 3:20 ESV*

The Lord showed up, knocking, so that, He could teach, orchestrate and show me I had a beautiful identity.

".... because of the tender mercy of our God, by which the rising sun will come to us from Heaven to shine on those living in darkness and in the shadow of death to guide our feet into the path of peace."

Luke 1:78-79 NIV

Luke 1:78-79 tells us that Jesus came to give light to those who sit in darkness. He guides their feet, to find the way to peace with God, a purpose, and true joy. Do you know how He does it? He gently pulls us to His Word, acquainting us with our salvation and His identity for us. Not my "worldly identity," but the identity He had in mind when He knitted me together in my mother's womb, forming my individual fingerprints.

I realize my pre-Jesus life was a continual process of trying to find an identity that would quench my thirst, but they all ran out of water. It was as if I was trying to fill and drink from a cup with a hole in the bottom. All my worldly identities, achievements or "that thing I do," which people knew me by all had time limits, and they all left me somewhat empty, thirsty, longing, and searching!

"Everyone who drinks this water will be thirsty again, but whoever drinks the water I give them will never thirst."

John 4:13-14

Our identities in Christ are eternal, no time limits. They are inherent, given by God.

Is it as hard for you as it is for me to wrap your mind around the idea that in the 7.442 billion (2016) people there are on earth, there are no two alike? I look at my son and my daughter and I am in awe of them. They are so precious, so divine, and so uniquely their own identity from the minute they were born. They are not my husband

and they are not me! They are a whole new creation! This got me curious about identical twins. I discovered that they come from the same fertilized egg and share the same genetic blueprint. To a standard DNA test, they are indistinguishable. However, even indistinguishable twins do not have matching fingerprints. WOW, their DNA is the same, but they do not have the same identity.

No two alike.

Our identities are this way, as well. Except, in Christ, they are not from our earthly mother and father. They are from our father in Heaven. They are not earned by achievement, performance, or title and they were specifically, individually, and lovingly handcrafted just for us. When someone gets to know the true identity of Jesus and their identity in Him, they create a Christ-centered life and He becomes their "watering hole and their oxygen to live on. He is the only possible thing that can fill the emptiness and truly quench the thirst of, *'Who am I?'*

Christ is the only possible thing that can fill the emptiness and truly quench the thirst of, 'Who am I?'

I was blessed once in the form of a vision from the Lord. It felt scary to have a vision! I long for that blessing again someday. It was God giving me my map to breakthrough.

I was being led in prayer by a mentor at the Women's Walk with Christ Retreat in Estes Park. (Side note, this retreat is sacred ya'll. The amount of prayer that goes into it is unreal! Prayer, prayer, and lots of prayer makes something as sacred as a vision possible.) As one of the women led me in prayer, she asked if I could see Jesus. I could. She asked me where he was.

"Is He in front of you, behind you, holding you? Is He close, is He far? What does He look like?"

He was in front of me. Not close. She asked me why He was not close was there something between Him and I.

Yes, there was a river between Him and I. He was beautiful. He was love, He was accepting, He was approachable, He was proud, and His arms reached out towards me.

What was the river like she asked me? Is there anything in the river?

There wasn't anything in the river, but there were things floating above the river . . . words, lots of words: Loved, Accepted, Enough, His, Sacred, Constant, Devine, Chosen, Abundance, Rest, Beauty, Comfort, Holy, Free, Goodness, Forgiven, Grace, Healthy, Whole, Fit, Compassion, Light, Daughter, Friendship, Wisdom, Gentleness, Righteous, Shepard, Justice, Kindness, Peace, Powerful, Refuge, Rest.

"Do any of them stand out to you?"

Yes, **OBEDIENCE** was in black, bold, capital letters. I didn't know what obedience meant that day, but I do now. He was saying, "You are seen, you are known, and you are loved. You are enough. Have obedience when I call you into your identity in Me and you will have complete access to my never-ending supply of water, love, grace, purpose, and true meaning."

As I got to know Jesus, His heart, His love, and His identity, He completely changed my perspective from *'Who am I?'* to *'I know who I am!'*

He took the "not" from my "not enough."

I went from this sucks to I am blessed.

I went from fearing this world's conditional love, to not caring because I am unconditionally loved by Jesus.

I went from thinking I might drown under the pressure of this world, to God will never let the waters sweep over me.

I went from being thirsty to, "My cup floweth over!"

Having a relationship with Jesus allows us to have an inexplainable peace when others don't, to find joy when others can't, and to experience rest for our minds, bodies, and souls, while others feel the weight of the world. He allows us to enjoy who we are created to be, imperfections and all. He also says, *'Know that I love you too much to leave you that way.'*

He knows our start and He knows our finish. He grows us up in between with spiritual formation so that we can start seeing God the way Jesus sees God and ourselves the way Jesus sees us and other people the way Jesus sees them.

Our true identities.

It's certainly not a conflict-free life, because Jesus doesn't promise anyone a storm-free life. He promises a storm-proof life and it's true! Now, when the weight of the world gets too heavy, Jesus picks up the slack. And I was wrong about Moses. He wasn't a physically, spiritually, and emotional strong enough man to do it alone. God was picking up his slack.

Jesus doesn't promise anyone a storm-free life.

I created a solution to my closet issue.

No more throwing my stuff on the floor and falling into bed unfulfilled . . . most of the time, I should say. Let's be honest; some days I still fall into bed with nothing left, but then I pray! I created a war room in my closet. It went from my place to hide, to a place where I could cry out to God, a place to quench my thirst of being somewhere else or doing something else by drinking Jesus, and a place to put my oxygen mask on so that I don't pass out and I can take care of and put my best foot forward with my family.

I did it. I took everything . . . and I mean everything . . . out of my closet. If I hadn't worn it or used it in the last year, it was out, gone, given away, or tossed. I painted the walls purple. I taped encouragements up: "Do not worry." "Learn to pray about everything." "Give thanks to God as you ask Him for what you need." I hung a beautiful, colorful, and prophetic frame. "Life is fragile, Handle with PRAYER." The picture has a jagged crack through its crisp white, and otherwise seemingly perfect frame. That's my favorite part, a reminder that I'm not the only thing whose life missed the fairy tale of being perfect.

I also keep colorful note cards that say Breathe, Enjoy, Joy, Notice, and Listen. I have wood décor reading, "May your arrow fly straight, and your aim be true," "Love never fails," and "Be the reason someone smiles today." Lastly, there are three picture frames. To be honest, the frames are *supposed to* have the pictures of my husband, my son, and my daughter in them, but who has time to print pictures? I know what the frames represent. They represent why I'm doing this, and who I'm doing it for. I'm doing it for Jesus, for them, for me!

On good days I start my day in my spiritual war room.

Satisfy us in the morning with your unfailing love, that we may sing for joy and be glad all our days.

◈ *Psalm 90:14 NIV*

I am a work in progress. God won't be finished creating a masterpiece out of me until He calls me home. I now have one source of unconditional love: Jesus. I feel loved, seen, and known. My burden feels lighter. *For my yoke is easy and my burden is light*, says Matthew 11:30. We must resolve to stop looking to other things to fill my identity cup. If we fill our cups with and drink Jesus, we can live life thru the conflicts with peace, love, worth and an identity in Christ.

One of the exercises I did when I was at that Women's Walk with Christ Retreat was an identity exercise. We were given two circle sheets of paper. One shiny, stainless, pure white. The other darker. We were instructed: "On the darker paper, write everything the world thinks of you and what the world makes you think and feel about yourself. This is your 'worldly identity.'"

On the pure white paper, we were told to write everything we knew that God knew about us, plus everything He thinks about you and has promised you. This was our "identity in Him."

While my darker, worldly identity told me I was: not enough, fear, anxiety, no good, loser, failure, weak, unlovable, worry, ugly, stupid, worthless, not worthy, fat, boring, and alone, my second page told me of my pure and true identity in Christ. In Him, I am chosen, favored, covered, enough, worthy of mercy, worthy of grace, forgiven, never alone, capable, free, created in God's image, known by God, named by God, called, in the midst of God, immovable, delighted in, brave, a warrior, capable of all things through Christ who strengthens me, accepted, saved by grace, loved, worth far more than rubies and pearls, beautiful, daughter of The King, and a beloved child of God. I know which one I want to believe and I know which one is easier to believe.

Our worldly identities are faulty. They have time limits, cups with holes in the bottom. If you place your worldly identity paper on top of your identity in Christ. You can't see it! Your true identity is lost, but if you continue to fill your identity cup with the water Jesus supplies, therefore putting your identity in Christ paper over your worldly identity, the messages from the world are still there, but they are faded, dulled, and quieted!

I keep fighting voices in my mind that say I'm not enough.
Every single lie that tells me I will never measure up.
Am I more than just the sum of every high and every low?
Remind me once again just who I am, because I need to know
You say I am loved when I can't feel a thing
You say I am strong when I think I am weak
You say I am held when I am falling short
When I don't belong, oh You say that I am Yours
And I believe what You say of me.
I believe
The only thing that matters now is everything You think of me
In You I find my worth, in You I find my identity.
❧ "You Say" By Jason Ingram, Paul Maybury, and Lauren Daigle

Arise and shine, for your light has come. The glory of the Lord is risen upon you.

꩜ Isaiah 60:1 NIV

Get up and radiate the love of God and fulfill the identity he created for you. Why? Because your light has already come (John 1:9). Jesus is the light that enlightens every person who comes into the world. Jesus already came. Arise and shine now, and when you do, His glory will be seen on you! If we shine in confidence of what Jesus has already done for us, is doing for us, and will do for us, He will add onto us the other things we need, but we can't just sit and wait. We have to get moving! We must identify who He created us to be because we are all God's people created to be His workers that bring glory to His Kingdom. He has set aside specific identities in Him for each of us to be able to complete our mission and purpose that He has set aside specifically for each of us.

I was lost. I was broken. I cared way too much about what other people thought of me and what I thought the world expected of me. I let my failure to that worldly identity weigh me down. They, the people of this world, never saw me and perhaps never will because they're broken, too. God's identity for us is truth. God sees us for who we really are; He sees our identities in Him.

I no longer try to quench my thirst of who am I with worldly identities. I drink Jesus; I fill my cup with His unconditional love and the worth He says I was created to have! I learn more and more each day about my identity in Christ, the divine identity He chose for me. I try hard now to put my worldly identity paper underneath my identity in Christ!

How cool is it that the same God who created the mountains, oceans and galaxies looked at you and thought the world needed one of you, too?

꩜ Author Unknown

BRENDA WEBER is a wife, missionary, and mother to children and fur-babies. In addition to her work in a pharmacy, she has spent much of her passion and energy working with Joshua Blahyi Ministries' project, Liberia's Hope. Liberia's Hope is an outreach ministry that was founded to change the lives of ex-child soldiers. Learn more at: **www.loveliberia.com**. Recently retired, Brenda and her husband packed up home, lives, and dogs to relocate to Washington. *"He is no fool who gives what he cannot keep to gain that which he cannot lose."* ~Jim Elliot

Breakthrough

7

THE GOD OF BREAKTHROUGHS

Brenda Weber

When I was twenty-two years old, my husband and I started a pharmacy, had our second baby, and moved all within the same month! I'm not sure what we were thinking, but we knew this was what God wanted us to do. We survived the first two years of business, remaining faithful in our tithing even though money was tight for our family. Within the first few years, God prospered our business and it steadily grew.

Early on, we realized this was not just a business for us, but a ministry. We knew when our customers were diagnosed with illnesses. Many times, we would pray for them in the pharmacy. Since we live in a very small town, our customers were like family.

One particular man was a diabetic. He came into the pharmacy one day to pick up prescriptions for a sore that had developed on his foot. Being diabetic, a sore can quickly become infected and this one had. He didn't respond to treatment and the wound became gangrenous. Within a short time, he became bedridden and depressed. After trying everything, he had several specialists tell him that they would have to amputate his foot. The surgery was scheduled for the following week.

While in church that Sunday, God spoke to me and told me to go pray for the diabetic. Immediately, thoughts entered my mind.

'He wasn't a Christian, I didn't know him well; what would he think when I told him God instructed me to do this?'

I tried to buy more time by telling the Lord that, "Yes;" I would go, but maybe Monday or Tuesday.

He said, "No, now!"

I cleaned up the dishes from lunch and picked up the phone to call the customer. I told him that God spoke to me in church and told me to come pray for him.

He seemed surprised but said, "Come on over."

I told my husband, Dave, that I was going over to pray for our customer.

He said, "You are?"

I told him, "I have to! The Lord is making me!"

He decided to come with me. When we arrived at the house, I told the man and his wife that God had spoken to me and asked me to pray for him. I wanted to explain that God could heal him and wanted to do so, but instead God led me to tell him the story of our children's hamster.

God had spoken to me and asked me to pray for him.

I shared with him that my children had a hamster named Templeton and, when the hamster was three-years old my son, Jake, brought him to me. Templeton was nearly dead. He was barely breathing and his eyes were clouded with no life in them. He had mucous coming out of his nose and mouth. I told Jake and my daughter, Jessie, that Templeton was an old hamster and it was just his time to die. I told them to hold him for a while and keep him warm until he passed away.

They both said, "Noooo! Call the doctor!"

We knew our vet well and to make it look like I was trying to do something, I made the call. He told me that hamsters only live two to three years and then they usually develop a respiratory disease and die. He said there was nothing we could do for him.

I relayed this to the kids and they said, "Mom! Pray for him!"

I tried to talk them out of it. I had always taught them about the power of prayer. I knew this would ruin their faith! I couldn't pray for him! I told Jake to wrap him in a washcloth to keep him warm and let him go to heaven. I gently took Templeton out of his cage and gave him to Jake to hold. While doing this Jake dropped poor dying Templeton on the floor!

My husband, being the sensitive guy he is, said, "Well he's dead now!"

This didn't help! Now I had two crying children begging me to pray for their tiny pet. I relented and laid my hand on the little creature and said a prayer. I was sure good old Templeton had brain damage from the fall, but I asked the Lord for help. I told the kids to put him back in his cage to rest. I didn't want them to watch Templeton die. We put him in his cage and left him. I was trying to distract the children to get their minds off their dying friend.

About ten minutes had passed when I heard a noise that sounded very much like the wheel spinning in Templeton's cage. We went running to see what it was. Low and Behold, there was Templeton running around in his wheel. His eyes were bright and he had no mucous coming out of his nose or mouth. He was the healthiest hamster I had ever seen!

I learned a couple valuable lessons that day. One: my kids had more faith in God than I did. It certainly was not my faith that healed that hamster. And two: what matters to us, matters to God.

I told this man with a gangrenous foot that if God was concerned about a hamster, how much more concerned would He be about him. My husband and I then laid hands on his foot and I prayed a simple prayer asking God to heal this man because He loved him. When I looked up, his wife was crying. She had never been a very open and friendly person, so I was a bit shocked when she hugged me tightly and thanked us. She said no one else had bothered to come. I literally saw her heart soften before my eyes.

A couple days later, our customer went in for his pre-op appointment. He was scheduled for the amputation the following day. When the doctor took off his bandages he was shocked at the improvement and he told him he was cancelling the surgery and they would see how it looked in a few more days. A week later, this man who had been bedridden, walked into the pharmacy using a walker. The surgery was permanently canceled! The next week, he came in using a cane, and the following week he was walking on his own with tennis shoes! He did a little dance in the pharmacy to show me how great his foot felt. I will never forget the smile on his face.

But our God is the God of breakthroughs, so He had more stories to show me....

I'm a light sleeper. Someone could drop a pin in my room in the middle of the night and I would wake up. One Sunday morning, my alarm was going off and I wouldn't wake up, so my husband started shaking me. I finally woke from the most realistic dream I have ever had. I'd been dreaming that my daughter, Jessie, was hit by a car and killed. We were at the funeral home picking out her casket. It was all so real! I had this hopeless, devastating feeling. Even after waking up, I couldn't shake this dream. I told my husband about it and we both prayed together. I continued praying while getting ready for church until I felt peace about it.

I was sure I was praying for my daughter's life.

After church, we were celebrating Jessie's birthday with family at our house. After cleaning up from dinner I realized that Jessie and my niece were missing. I was told they went for a bike ride. I immediately remembered the dream and was overcome with fear. I was getting ready to go look for them when I saw them coming down the street on the bicycles. I was so relieved and thankful! I didn't give it much thought the rest of the day, but I didn't let my daughter leave on her bike again.

That evening, my sister called. She asked me if Jessie had told me what happened that day while the kids were on their bike ride.

I told her, "No."

She said, "Jessie was almost hit by a car!"

Right away, I went to Jessie and asked what happened. She told me that she wanted to take her cousin to see where we were building our new home. We had the foundation done and some of the walls had started going up. They had to cross a fairly busy highway to get to our new subdivision. In the area where they crossed, the speed limit went down to forty miles per hour from a fifty-mile-per-hour zone and there was a hill, which created a blind spot. My niece was ahead of her and had already crossed the highway. As my daughter started to cross, she heard a car coming. She looked up to see that a car was about to hit her. She had no time to react. She froze and closed her eyes waiting for the impact. When nothing happened, she opened her eyes. The car had come to a stop only a couple inches from her. There were no skid marks. The car just stopped. The lady, who was clearly shaken up, shouted at her for riding out into the road.

As Jessie was telling me about this I had a vision of a huge angel putting his hand out and stopping that car. I knew then, that this was the reason for the dream. The devil was going to try and take her life and I needed to pray extra hard for her protection. I have never disregarded a vivid dream like that after that day. I have come to know the difference between a normal dream and a spiritual dream and I take them very seriously.

But our God is the God of breakthroughs, so He had more stories to show me....

Six years ago, I turned fifty. Although I've accomplished a lot in that time, I felt there was something else, something bigger that God wanted me to do. My husband and I have been involved helping a pastor in Liberia, West Africa since 1999. We met the pastor, our friend, Josiah Swen, through our good friends that had a grandfather and grandmother who were missionaries in Liberia, until civil war broke out and

I felt there was something else, something bigger that God wanted me to do.

they were forced to return to the United States. We helped fund the construction of a church and school in Josiah's community. Through our relationship with Josiah and his family, I was aware of the horrific fourteen-year civil war and had heard stories of rebel generals and the child soldiers. The stories of these warlords were horrendous.

Fourteen years after meeting Josiah, my sister told me about a documentary she had watched about a particularly brutal rebel general. The documentary was called, *"The Redemption of General Butt Naked."* I watched as the story of an infamous warlord, named Joshua Blahyi, unfolded. He received his nickname, General Butt Naked, because he believed that if he went into battle naked he would be protected from bullets. It also struck fear into the hearts of everyone who saw him in battle. He, like several other rebel generals, would abduct teens and boys as young as eight-years-old forcing them to fight in the war. Usually the parents would be killed in front of them, so they were too terrified to go against them and thought they had no other choice but to join the rebels. They would be given drugs so that they were addicted and easy to control. The drugs had the ability to make them fearless fighters, and the warlords used that to their advantage. In the documentary, I watched

106

this rebel general speak about the atrocities he inflicted on the Liberian people.

I also listened to him speak about meeting Jesus in person during battle, and how that led to giving his life to Christ and changing the course of his existence. After the end of the war, he went into hiding outside of Liberia. During this time, he made the decision that he would return to Liberia and face the Truth and Reconciliation Committee (TRC) to answer for his part in the war.

Knowing he could be hanged, he returned to Liberia. He was the only rebel general to voluntarily do this. He confessed that he was directly or indirectly responsible for more than 20,000 deaths. Seeing he was a changed man, the TRC recommended him for amnesty. Back in Liberia, he sought out to help those he had hurt during the war. He went to the families of those who were hurt and asked for their forgiveness, offering his help in any way he could. I saw those people soften and forgive him. Joshua, the given name he took up once more, then devoted his life to making up for his mistakes. He wanted to start a home where he could take in ex-child soldiers, who were now young men, with plans to rehabilitate them. He spent countless hours going into the ghettos to preach God's love to the people there. I was so struck by Joshua's story that I wanted to help.

He wanted to start a home....

There are no social programs in Liberia to help these men who are traumatized, addicted to drugs, and forced to live in the ghettos where they survive by stealing. I wanted to reach out to this changed warlord. With my contacts in Liberia, I thought I could help Joshua with his ministry somehow. I found him on Facebook and sent him a message. He responded immediately. We messaged back and forth and then he called me. The call ended up being a two-hour conversation, during which I prayed for him and shared the vision God was giving me. The vision was of a huge compound surrounded by jungle. I told him this would be his mission compound with housing, a church, school, and clinic. There was a training center where men were being taught a trade. Joshua was so excited because he had been given the same vision by God years earlier. He was currently at the point of giving up. Through trying to minister to these young men, he had lost his wife and was in fear of losing his children. He was discouraged and ready to give up when I contacted him. He told me that he had two and a half acres of land outside Monrovia.

I said, "Joshua, what God showed me was hundreds of acres of land out in the jungle, I think He has more in store!"

We both realized that our meeting was not an accident and I've been involved ever since. In 2012, with the help of a pastor from New York, we started a formal ministry. We took eighteen young men from the ghetto to get them off drugs, rehabilitate them, and teach them a trade. It was a yearlong program. The hard part was picking only eighteen of the hundreds that wanted our help.

In January of 2013, I took my first trip to Liberia. It was finally time to meet my brother, Joshua, and my guys! I had photos of each of them and had memorized their names and faces. My family was not thrilled, to say the least. I believe the word "crazy" was used to describe the trip. I suppose traveling to a war-torn country to hang out with an ex-rebel general and thieves from the worst ghetto in the world does sound a bit nuts!

So, I said, "I'll take my sister with me!"

To my surprise, she actually said yes. She is four years older than me and not quite as adventurous, or at least wasn't at that time! This is the sister who was afraid to go kayaking in the backwaters of Georgia because she thought an alligator would get her and we were about to go to a country with the most poisonous snakes in the world! But her love for me wouldn't allow me to go alone. She thought we might die, but she wouldn't let me die alone! That January, two white women, fifty and fifty-four years old, from the U.S., headed to a war-torn country to meet up with one of the most notorious warlords in Liberian history. We arrived in Liberia and walked off the plane into what felt like a sauna! When we left O'Hare it was -35 degrees Fahrenheit! Climate shock was added to culture shock.

All this was forgotten when we got through customs and headed out of the airport into the best welcoming party we had ever had! Our guys were singing, dancing, and hugging us. Everyone at the airport thought we were American celebrities! I greeted each one by name. They were so excited that I knew their names! My sister and I instantly fell in love with these guys! Any fear we had of the unknown quickly disappeared with the outpouring of love we received from these wonderful young men. We gained eighteen sons that day.

Over the course of a week, our lives changed. Suddenly, the things that once felt important were quickly put into perspective. We saw people who worked from sun up to sun down just to feed their families. We met women whose children had starved to death or died from very treatable childhood illnesses.

Over the course of a week, our lives changed

The thing about these wonderful people was that, in the midst of this difficult life, there was joy on their faces. We spent a lot of time getting to know our guys. While most of them were well into their twenties, they seemed like little boys. Every once in a while, an argument broke out over whose turn it was to hold our hands! We laughed so hard at their antics. We also cried as we heard horrific stories of their tragic young lives.

One story I will never forget was from a young man named David. One day, his captain and a couple other soldiers saw a pregnant woman and were placing bets on whether she was going to have a boy or a girl. When the bets were placed, they brought David over. He was only around nine at the time. They asked David whether he thought she was going to have a boy or a girl. He proudly made his guess. The captain then handed him a machete and he was forced to cut open the belly of the young women to see who won the bet.

David was never the same after that. Just when we thought we had heard the worst story we had ever heard, we would hear another one. It would be easy to focus only on these horrific stories, but the love and laughter of these damaged young men wouldn't allow us to do that.

One day we decided to take around 230 young men and women from the ghetto on an outing to the beach. West Point ghetto is known as one of the worst ghettos in the world. I can't imagine living there. We rented a bus and took them out of the ghetto for the afternoon. We fed them and preached God's love and forgiveness to them. After lunch, one of my sweet guys brought a young man to me who had a bad wound on his leg. I only had a small first aid kit with me, but cleaned the wound the best I could with what I had. I bandaged him with sterile gauze and Neosporin ointment. Next, they brought a girl who had a similar wound. I repeated the process.

Then a young boy came up to me and said, "Mama Brenda, I have a wound too", I asked him to see his wound. He showed me a tiny scratch on his leg. I gently placed on a bandage and his face lit up. To him the band-aid was not just a bandage; it was love.

After that, we were accepted into the ghetto family. They could see our hearts by this simple act. You see, the people who live in the ghetto are like lepers, outcasts of society; no one touches them, especially white women from America. At the end of the outing we asked who would be interested in

The people who live in the ghetto are like lepers, outcasts of society.

going through our rehabilitation program. Every one of them said yes! It was clear we needed a bigger home! A couple days later we left Liberia, a country and people we had grown to love. Even though we were going home, we also felt like we were leaving home. We would never be the same. These beautiful people had become our family and this tiny country in West Africa had become our second home.

We are still working towards our goal of a larger facility and I believe it's only a matter of time before I see God's vision for the ministry fulfilled.

> *After all, our God is the God of breakthroughs and I know He has more stories to show me....*

MARIA NOTCH is a #1 Best-Selling Author and speaker. Driven by her love for people and her love of the Lord, she walks with women experiencing infertility, miscarriage, or loss of a child, as well as those growing their families. Her blog educates people about challenges in these areas, supports those who are hurting, and brings awareness to the community. Maria serves on staff at her church in the music ministry and as the director of the Milwaukee Mercy Choir. Maria is married to her high school sweetheart, Jacob, and is mommy to LJ, MaryAnne, and four babies in Heaven. For more information about Maria and her ministries or speaking visit: **Hopeandhealing.blog.**

Breakthrough

8

THE NAME OF LIGHT

Maria Notch

M y husband and I had been living in darkness for years. After the birth of our son, we miscarried three babies in an eighteen-month period. I battled major depression, our marriage faced its most challenging chapter, and our son—in his loneliness—longed desperately for a sibling. Although we had the joy of the Lord in our hearts, our eyes were veiled by the darkness we felt.

We embarked on an extensive medical journey that included two surgeries, countless hormone therapies, and painful injections; the journey spanned over two years. My incredible team of doctors helped us discover that I had low progesterone and estradiol, a blood clotting disorder that only showed up when I was pregnant, a genetic mutation, and widespread endometriosis. After addressing each of those issues and completely overhauling my diet, I finally reached a physically healthy place. My husband and I could say with confidence that both of our bodies were the strongest they'd ever been and everything was "working properly." Yet mysteriously, we seemed to have lost the ability to conceive. This was a problem we'd never faced in our entire married life, and it was wearing on us.

We found ourselves in the fall of 2017 sitting around a campfire wondering what the Lord could be up to and pondering adoption. This was something we'd been open to throughout our married life, but it was never a burning desire on our hearts. As the fire crackled and sparks flew, Jacob and I threw out questions like, *'Domestic or international? Infant or toddler? American, European, or African?'*

For once in our seven years of marriage, we found ourselves on the exact same page. (We are the epitome of opposites attracting, yet this time God brought our hearts and minds to the same conclusions.) Our joint agreement to enter the journey of adoption left us staring into the flames, mesmerized, bewildered, and a bit curious at the possibility of becoming adoptive parents.

God brought our hearts and minds to the same conclusions.

Something shifted in us that night.

We decided that if we were not pregnant by the new year, then we would pursue adoption. I went from being devastated every month when I would start a new cycle, to feeling ecstatic that we were one month closer to adopting. God was building the desire in me. In November, when we intentionally shifted the focus of our prayers, our confidence grew rapidly that God was hearing and would answer us! When I got my period in December, I had a supernatural peace and told Jacob that "someone else is carrying our baby." What a strange thing to say when still trying to conceive! But, in all honesty, there was a part of our hearts that knew we were going to have another baby . . . and that this next one wasn't going to be our biological child.

At Christmas, we shared our plans with our families, and—despite our confidence and excitement about adoption—we battled unforeseen jealousy by being around other family members who were expecting. Two of the women closest to me were both pregnant and due the next summer. The ultimate test of my faith was striving to rejoice with them, while setting aside my feelings of envy because they were able to carry their babies.

The first of the year arrived and we were not pregnant, so we started telling everyone about our desire to adopt. Within that first week of January, as I shared with one woman who often counseled me, she mentioned a young girl she knew who was pregnant and unable to keep her baby.

'Wouldn't that be crazy?' we thought, as we wondered if God would connect the two of us so early in this process. Jacob and I prayed fervently that whole month that this girl would choose life for her child and would not abort. What a blessing it was to pray for them, whether the baby would become a part of our forever family or not. We found out later that an abortion had been scheduled, but this young mother woke up the morning of the appointment saying she couldn't abort. After learning that, we knew God had a special calling on this little one, and felt even more privileged to be able to pray for this mother and her unborn baby!

February arrived, and our mutual friend continually asked me for a bio, website, or something she could show to this young mom to introduce her to our family. So we launched JacobandMaria-adopt.com specifically for this expectant mother to see, but shared it with the rest of the world on social media, as well. The outpouring of support we got was overwhelming. Very few people knew about this young mother, but everyone in our lives was ecstatic at the prospect of us growing our family through adoption! That month, this expectant mother viewed our page, liked what she saw (especially our son and our Disney pictures), and stated that—after she found out the sex of the baby—she wanted to meet us.

If you're at all like me, it concerned me that she wanted to wait to discover the sex. *'Would she keep the baby if it was a girl? How does that impact her decision to parent or place?'* These were the kinds of things I wondered. Our mutual friend assured me, "she wants to tell you, *'This is a little boy,'* or, *'This is a little girl for your family.'"*

This left me speechless ."Did she really say that?" I asked.

Yes, she did. That was when it hit me that we might actually match with this expectant mom. But that is also when the ultimate test of our faith and the toughest waiting period began.

For a couple months, we didn't hear anything and we began to wonder if she'd changed her mind, especially considering she was well past the twenty-week point in her pregnancy when she could find out the gender. We continued praying for her, her pregnancy, and her baby. At times, we

We dared to hope that God was orchestrating something incredible.

doubted if anything would come of this. Other times, we dared to hope that God was orchestrating something incredible. All along, though, it felt as if God were asking us to walk by faith and not by sight. So we kept preparing to adopt, even though it felt like we were walking in that direction blindfolded.

Our life continued moving forward. Work kept my husband and me busy, plus he was in school and had night classes twice a week. Going to continuous doctor's appointments seemed like another full-time job for me, as I was still doing all my fertility treatments in addition to being mom to a five-year-old.

Our son was in school when, on the last Wednesday of April, my phone rang. It was our mutual friend, who only ever texts and had never called me. I was in a work meeting, so I sent it to voicemail. It wasn't until it rang a second time, only a minute later, that I remembered *'It's Wednesday the 25th! She's meeting with that expectant mom today!'* I quickly excused myself from the meeting and answered the phone.

My friend told me that this pregnant mom was sitting there with her and that she wanted to meet our family. Only a moment later, I found myself talking with this woman I'd prayed for over the last many months. As she picked up the phone she said "I hear you want a girl. Well it just so happens that I'm pregnant with a girl!"

Imagine yourself on the phone with a woman you have never met. Without even knowing you, she's basically pointing to the greatest desire of your heart, and saying, "Here, you can have it." What do you say? How do you feel? What is your response?

For me, all I could say was, "That's amazing!" Because how else do you respond when someone basically says you can have the baby she has been nourishing in her own body. This expectant mom went on to say, "I don't want to toot my own horn, but I make beautiful babies!" It was at that moment I knew we were going to be friends!

Our conversation continued as she told me a bit about herself and her older daughter, who was turning six just two days later. My mind went blank as she invited us to the birthday party that Friday night!

"Of course we can come! We'd love to!" I responded, as I couldn't think of anything more important than meeting the woman who could possibly be our daughter's birthmom. It was a pleasant surprise to hear that her six-year-old's favorite things were Paw Patrol and Legos™, same as our son. We committed to meeting at the party that weekend!

As I hung up the phone, my heart nearly exploded, first out of sheer excitement and then out of sheer panic, as I looked at my calendar and realized I was scheduled to lead the worship team at our church's Confirmation Mass that Friday night! I'd completely forgotten and honestly was torn about what to do; do I honor my commitment to work, or put my family and ministering to this expectant mother first? Well, God made it abundantly clear as my top pick for a substitute was available and willing to come serve that night in my absence. The entire team stepped up and covered me so that I could focus on my family and who God put in front of us that night: this expectant mother and her six-year-old.

Such excitement and anticipation filled those next two days. Shopping for the birthday girl was a blast, and we explained to our son that he was going to make a new friend and celebrate her on her birthday! We mentioned that her mommy had a baby in her tummy and it didn't faze him. Although he prayed every night for "God to send us another baby in mommy's tummy or one that we can adopt," he was used to being around all my pregnant friends and the young, expectant moms at church to whom I ministered. We wanted to be cautious to guard his little heart in case this pairing didn't pan out.

I journaled as we drove to the party that Friday, and it felt like our lives were about to change. It was the same feeling I had years ago when journaling an hour before my husband proposed to me! I wanted to capture the emotions, the thoughts, and the conversations that surrounded the evening. Before we got out of the car I said to my husband, "Even if nothing comes of this, I'm thankful for you and our son and I'm good if it's just us for the rest of our lives."

It felt like our lives were about to change.

God had other plans. As soon as we walked into the hotel pool party, this beautiful pregnant woman walked up to us, introduced herself, and looking at our son, promptly told her daughter, "you're going to be seeing a lot of him." That was the first indication that her mind was made up. She was placing this baby for adoption, and we were the family she had chosen. A little while later, another school mom showed up to the party. She asked the birthmom "What do you all need before the baby arrives?" I watched as our birthmother took a deep breath, looked over at me, and then replied, "I'm actually putting her up for adoption . . . and this is the family," as she pointed in our direction. We were swimming in the pool at the time and I seriously wanted to go under the water, scream, do a happy dance, and maybe drown out the disbelief. Instead, I swam over to relieve her of the awkwardness and introduce myself to the school mom. That was our breakthrough moment.

As the night went on, we got to know her, some of her family, and her daughter. At one point out of the blue she told me, "I'm due July 24th, but I'm scheduled for a C-section a week early. So you should plan for that." Once again, my mind was blown at the conversation we were having! Jacob and I went into the night anticipating this as a casual get-to-know-you and "see if this is a good fit" kind of meeting. She went in, it seemed, knowing she wanted to place her baby in our family.

We drove home stunned that evening. With our son sitting in the backseat, we had to be coded with our conversations because, again, we wanted to guard his heart. I called a few women - namely, the lady who introduced us to this gal, my mom, my mother-in-law, and my mentor. As luck would have it, my mentor (and spiritual mother) has worked in the adoption world for over twenty years.

I remember her saying to me, "As far as birthmothers ago, this gal sounds like her mind is made up. She is placing this baby for adoption and you are the family."

My husband and I process things quite differently - I'm an extrovert and he's an introvert. When we got home, he promptly went to bed, whereas I was so excited I couldn't sleep! Both of us spent that weekend planning the next steps we needed to take because the birthmom was due in twelve short weeks. We simultaneously began interviewing multiple adoption agencies and created a go fund me page to fund raise the daunting cost of adoption, which we now needed to have within the next three months!

Those next few weeks were comprised of a series of miracles and perfectly timed events! God clearly closed the doors to certain agencies and flung wide open the doors to others. My mentor, who works in the industry, gave me the name of one agency that she thought would be a good fit for us. It turned out that, to apply with them, we had to attend an informational meeting first. I spoke with them on a Monday, and their next meeting happened to be the very next day!

Additionally, we were going to need to apply to the agency and pay for our home study. We knew when you add in the upfront lawyer fees, as well as birth parent service, the cost was astronomical. If something were to change and this expectant mom were to make a different decision, our costs would double overnight. We'd saved and budgeted for adoption, but we anticipated a one to three *year* timeline, not one to three *months*!

We humbled ourselves and fundraised. This was a difficult decision for both of us, and one for which we even took some flack. Nonetheless, I kept saying to my husband, "At the end of the day, this baby girl needs a home. And we've been chosen! So who are we to be too proud to ask for help to make this happen." God

God blessed our obedience and showed up through His people in a big way.

blessed our obedience and showed up through His people in a big way. Within one week, we had enough to cover all of our initial costs!

It was incredible to experience the outpouring of love and support through prayers and financial generosity. I was sitting at the informational meeting with our adoption agency, knowing I needed several hundred dollars for the application, when a notification popped up on my phone that a couple from church just donated . . . several hundred dollars. Cue the waterworks! Another day, we found out our lawyer fees were due much sooner than anticipated. I had just told my mother-in-law that I didn't know where the funds were going to come from, when a huge donation came in that night! Again, I turned into a blubbering mess. The Lord continuously showed us

His faithfulness and assured us that He was in every detail, which was our daily prayer!

While this was happening, I was preparing mentally and emotionally for my next meeting with our birthmom. We were getting together, along with our mutual friend, to talk through details. The night before we met, my husband pulled me aside and said "I think we should slightly change the name we have picked out for our baby girl, and I'm only telling you this because I think it's going to come up in conversation tomorrow."

We had had the name Marian Thérèse chosen since we were pregnant with our son six years earlier, but my husband suggested we change it to MaryAnne Thérèse in honor of her birthmom. Sure enough, when we met the next day, the birthmom brought up the topic of baby names in conversation, and I was able to share the name we had in mind for our baby girl.

It was at that get-together that she *officially* asked us to adopt her daughter. In fact, she did so in such a beautiful way. Rubbing her belly, she asked us, "Would you like to be a part of our family?"

I answered with an emphatic, "Of course. We'd be honored!" That day, we also discovered breastfeeding was important to both of us, and she fully supported me in inducing lactation to feed our daughter. (Science is truly a blessing from God!) We officially paired, and many other details came together.

Jacob and I began what would be a ten-week home study. We were in the middle of a major basement demolition. I worked tirelessly ahead at work to prepare for a maternity leave as we anticipated growing our family. We met again with the birthmom, this time out for a nice dinner without the kids. Our conversations flowed naturally and were governed by openness and honesty. She shared how, in order to place the baby in our home, she needed the few days in the hospital, but that we were welcome to be there and share in the experience. Although we were nervous she might go into labor early, she made it to the day of her scheduled C-section.

We connected over the phone the night before delivery to go over some final details of the plan, and she agreed to text us once baby was born so we could come meet her. After hours of delays at the hospital, our daughter was born on Tuesday, July 17th, 2018 at 12:25 P.M. By that evening, we were meeting her, giving her a first bath, and loving on both her and her birthmom. Two days later, we brought our son in to meet her, and one of the most precious moments was watching him sign and sing *Jesus Loves Me* to the baby girl he hoped would be his little sister.

Mentally, I knew that my priority those four days in the hospital was to be about supporting and encouraging birthmom so that she could make the best decision for herself and her child. With that in mind, I didn't allow myself to think of this beautiful baby girl as "ours" until we left the hospital with her. Those days were the most difficult and yet most beautiful throughout this process. It was such an honor to get to walk with our birthmom throughout that time and witness her strength and love for this little one. It was also incredibly challenging to literally "share" a baby and walk the fine line between being a friend to the birthmom and a prospective adoptive parent to the baby. Again, because of our open and honest relationship, she was able to voice her needs and, oftentimes, when she needed alone time with the baby, it proved a blessing to us to be able to have a break from the intensity.

My husband was a rock for both of us mamas through those days. One of the most touching moments was when the birthmom made him promise to take this sweet baby girl out on dates when she grew up! Oh did I cry! He listened when I needed to process. He made us all laugh when we needed to laugh. He took our five-year-old son and birth mom's six-year-old daughter out for walks when we needed quiet. And he loved like our great Heavenly Father loves.

The last night the birthmom had with baby, she asked to have alone with her family. We were happy to honor her wishes and had a "normal" family night out at a t-ball game. In hindsight, it was our last night as a family of three. We called our priest to come over for some extra "spiritual support" and some drinks to keep our minds off of what was at stake the next morning. He honestly got us over the hump (and three days later he was back at our home meeting our daughter).

When we walked into the hospital the next morning, I asked my husband, "What are the chances that we walk out of here today with a baby? 50/50?"

He told me he thought we were looking at an 80/20 chance. That went up to almost 100% certainty after we saw and spoke with the birthmom. She exuded immense strength and a selfless love like I've never witnessed before. She was honest and vulnerable about how challenging this was, yet unwavering in her decision. There was never a doubt she loved this little girl and wanted what was best for her.

> *The birthmom exuded immense strength and a selfless love like I'd never witnessed before.*

At 3:00 in the afternoon on Friday, July 20th, the birthmom said her goodbyes, buckled baby girl into our car, and we headed home. It took me until we were about halfway home to stop crying, because my heart was truly breaking for this woman I had grown to love and respect. That's when I knew I'd done a good job focusing on her and not just the baby throughout those days in the hospital. I finally snapped out of it when I realized she would be so mad at me if she knew I was crying for her sake versus switching into mom mode for our baby's sake . . . *our baby.*

Bringing MaryAnne home to our five-year-old and snuggling on the couch *alone* for the first time as a family of four was so surreal. Our son had a present for his new baby sister, and she (with our help) had Legos™ for him! They exchanged gifts and then MaryAnne got hungry.

"Time for her and mommy to get to know each other," my husband told me.

So I took her into the bedroom, went skin to skin, and she latched right on! Remember earlier I mentioned how breastfeeding was so important to me and the birthmom? Well, I had been taking a medication and pumping around the clock for a month leading up to delivery. I knew my milk had come in, but I didn't know how baby would latch until after we got home. Praise God, she nursed like a champ, and we've been breastfeeding ever since! It is by far one of the most beautiful details of this whole process and absolutely key in bonding. Ladies, we have superpowers stamped into our bodies, designed by God himself to be nurturing and life-giving!

With an open adoption, the birthmom and the adoptive family stay in touch, and the child grows up knowing his or her biological parents, or the birthmom, in this case. She scheduled a joint family photo shoot for all of us the week after delivery. It was a nice thing for all of us to look forward to! It was a chance for her to see baby again and a special way to capture our two families coming together.

In the five weeks between discharge from the hospital and our court date, we gave MaryAnne all the love we had! We treated her the same as if she were our biological daughter. If anything, we loved on her extra, because we knew we were not guaranteed anything. We had her on what's called a legal risk placement, in that the birth mom was still the legal guardian, and we were

We loved on MaryAnne extra because we knew we were not guaranteed anything.

essentially functioning as foster parents for that month . . . all the way up until August 24th; that's when our TPR (Termination of Parental Rights) court hearing was scheduled.

The week of court, I was so nervous, because I understood the how high the stakes were. I had come to love this little girl with my whole heart and the thought of losing her was unbearable. The morning of the 24th, I took her to Mass with me and thought, *'Lord, if this is the last day I have with her, I want to bring her to You.'* As most other days when we took her to church, she got the biggest smile on her face! It was like she knew she was home in her Father's House!

> *I had come to love this little girl with my whole heart and the thought of losing here was unbearable.*

As with everything else leading up to this, the birthmom remained steadfast in her decision. Despite the judge and the lawyer having to thoroughly grill her to maintain she was in sound mind and body and understood fully what she was doing, she stuck with her decision to place MaryAnne in our home.

I thought everything would hit me at that point and my emotions would get the best of me that night or that weekend. Surprisingly, my mind and heart took longer to catch up to reality. It wasn't until a week or two after court, when I least expected it, that the emotions would wash over me and I'd become completely overwhelmed. After one particular 4:00 A.M. feeding, MaryAnne had a full tummy. She smiled at me and giggled for fifteen minutes straight. It finally hit me – I'm her mommy and she knows it. It took until that moment to allow myself to feel loved *in return* by this little one. Finally, I was able to bask in and enjoy this mother-daughter relationship, free from fear or insecurities.

After our miscarriages, my arms used to physically ache to hold a baby. I think of that often now as I hold my rainbow baby in my arms. A rainbow baby is that which follows a loss . . . the promise that comes after the storm. Although my arms don't ache anymore, I'll never forget the storm or the darkness that consumed me. I will, however, be forever grateful for the bright, shining light that broke through the darkness!

That light's name is MaryAnne.

Personal Responsibility

This one's a biggie. Here is why—because a victim will NEVER experience breakthrough. Never.

I promise you, if you believe you are a victim of everyone else's choices and that you have no choices left for yourself, breakthrough is not in your future. However, if you stop the finger-pointing and take total responsibility for your life and the condition it is in today, including the choices you made to get you here, then you are on your way. Taking responsibility is freeing! It opens up options for us. By owning that we helped make a problem, that means that we can help solve it! (Thank God!) Breakthrough happens when we take 100% responsibility for our:

ACTIONS	ATTITUDES
HABITS	DREAMS
EMOTIONS	DESIRES
RESPONSES	HEALTH
DECISIONS	FINANCES
MOODS	TIME

Simply said, taking full responsibility is choosing to focus on and keep *your* side of the street clean despite what others are choosing to do with their side. That means you are *more concerned with your mess than someone else's.* If we do not own the fact that our side of the street has some garbage on it, we will never get out of our pity parties and go grab that much needed broom.

By taking 100% ownership of our lives and choices, we stop the powerless victim mindset dead in its tracks and open the door of opportunity for real and lasting change and a life we can enjoy!

Reji Laberje is the Writing and Publishing Coach for FEW. She's published more than fifty books and plays, traditionally and independently, including nine #1 Bestsellers. Reji has helped nearly fifty authors become #1 Bestsellers. She teaches, writes, edits, consults and coaches, does layout, and markets for traditional and nontraditional publishers, classes, and authors of sportswriting, biography, leadership, juvenile fiction and nonfiction, self-improvement, Christian writing, and playwriting. While in her third decade as a writer, her roles in the industry pale to those of Christian, veteran, wife, and mother. With her close-knit family, friends, and loved ones, she enjoys service, music, lake life, theatre, games, camping, football (Go Bears!), travel, her pets, and life in beautiful Wisconsin. Learn more about Reji, her books, writing coaching, and her online courses at: **www.bucketlisttobookshelf.com**.

Breakthrough
9

MOTHERS, DAUGHTERS, ATHEISTS,

AND CHANGING PERSPECTIVES

Reji Laberje

I was raised as an atheist.

That was how I began my testimony every time I gave it. I'm going into my tenth year as a Christian now, although it's getting harder to remember the time before I knew—deep in every part of my being— what the truth really was. Nonetheless, for the first thirty-three years of my life, I was not just an atheist; I was an adamant, hard-headed atheist. I was the atheist who knew the Bible well enough to debate you on it by pulling verses out of context to put you in your place, despite the fact that I didn't have the wisdom of Biblical understanding, yet. I was the atheist who worked hard to convince people that you could not be educated *and* believe the "fairy tales" of Christianity. (Yes, I see the ignorance now; science only proves the Bible.) I was proud of my beliefs, "better" for them, holding passionately to the false opinion that they were correct, and buying into the idea that Christians were, as I had been taught: stupid, weak, or brainwashed. Ultimately, atheism failed for me. After all, *in the end*, it always will . . . for everyone.

I'm not here to tell the story of how that happened. In fact, I'm done telling that story. There are plenty of people *new* to the faith to tell their *new* stories of finding *new* life in Christ. The story of how I became a Christian would be irrelevant – if I had stopped growing as one on the day I took the plunge and chose to get baptized. You see,

The story of how I became a Christian would be irrelevant. . . .

because of my atheism, I felt for years that my testimony was awfully special. More than special. I thought it was a miracle. And the fact that I got baptized at age thirty-three made me feel all the more prideful about my personal transformation, because after all, Jesus had thirty-three years to fulfill his purpose, so I felt I had this timeline in common with Him. Wow! I could never have been more right . . . and more wrong . . . at the same time.

Of course my change of heart and discovered belief were miracles. That's where I was right. Every soul saved is a miracle. But prideful? Smug, even (I'll admit it.) over being saved? How ridiculous! It's not as if I really had anything to do with it! Being prideful over finding Christ is like being proud of a meal you had nothing to do with preparing. All I did was . . . *finally, after countless invitations* . . . pull up a chair to the table. That table? Yeah. I had nothing to do with setting that, either. So what on Earth was I taking pride in? It should not have been pride, rather it should have been humility. Humility in this new life was something that would take a decade to grow. Christianity isn't just a one-time decision through baptism, it's a daily choice to be filled with the Holy Spirit and a lifelong process of maturing in the faith. I didn't get all of that yet.

After my baptism, and the subsequent baptisms of my husband and children, I became very quickly and passionately involved in my church, service work, missions, ministry, and teaching through groups and classes; I even reshaped my business to ensure it was God-honoring and was as much a mission field as anyplace I served within the church. I now knew I had the answers that everybody was seeking and needed to feel complete, live on purpose, love on others, and impact the world positively. In these various outlets, there were always opportunities to share truth and how I came to it. These stories are real and raw and meaningful. I do not mean to disparage that reality. Certainly, stories of how people learn the truth of who God is and who we are in Christ is something that has genuine eternal value. You never know when a piece of your history will speak to somebody else who is feeling uncertain about who God is, how powerful He can be, of His healing and – just as importantly – fulfilment and prosperity that come through a life with Him. This is why we tell our stories. It is for those souls we can reach through the relatability found in our own life tales. I do not wish to discourage the telling of testimonies. I want only to make sure that we don't stop writing our stories on the day our names are written in God's book. I did just that without even realizing it.

Don't stop writing our stories on the day our names are written in God's book.

Because of my upbringing, I had all sorts of ugly stories about who I was for a very long time. I didn't like that person much. I also had stories about the people I blamed for making me that way. Primarily, this fell on my parents, and in particular, my mother. Good or bad, it always comes down to our mothers, doesn't it? I butted heads with mine for as long as I could remember. The two of us were, and continue to be, alike in a lot of ways. We both fight passionately, love achingly, and feel deeply. We have similar tastes in music, art, home, and even style. Believe me, as I grow older, I see more of my mom in the mirror each day than I do of myself. Also, for most of my life, our atheism was something we shared, too.

Despite our similarities, we were very *different* in the ways that we lived as these emotional beings. I trusted loosely. My mother was more cautionary with people. My life has always been tornadic; in schedule, relationships, career, and my home. My mother likes order, control, structure, and organization. And don't even get me started on individual issues. We've stood on opposite sides of just about every major political and culturally or socially controversial topic for the past thirty years of my life, long before we had faith as a difference.

To say we fought and fought often is a serious understatement. From nasty or passive-aggressive asides to full blowouts, from the time I was fifteen until I was well into my thirties, our relationship was contentious at the best of times, and not uncommonly hostile. My mom fought dirty. Though, I imagine if you ask her, she likely believes I did the same. Perspective is funny that way. If you hold up a penny between two people, one will always see the head and the other will always see the tail. From their unique points-of-view, they're both right, both wrong, and both frustrated that the other could possibly call a tail a head . . . or a head a tail.

If you hold up a penny between two people, one will always see the head and the other will always see the tail.

Not long after getting baptized, my mother and I had a fight. *Shocker.* It was one of the big ones. We've only had five of the "big ones" in my entire adulthood. Every couple of years, we would decide to go in for another round with one another, and verbally slug it out to inflict the most harm possible. From my *perspective* (there's that pivotal word again), I felt like my mom had never done right following any of the other blowups. It seemed I was the one who would always forgive and accept her back into my life without the problem ever having been resolved or apologized for. She'd suffered from mental illness (manic depression and obsessive-compulsive disorder) after many genuine traumas in her life, so she wasn't capable of knowing the hurt she caused, sometimes even forgetting the things that she had verbally inflicted in the heat of the moment. It's a real thing – blacking out as a result of mental overdrive. And it's something you begrudgingly grow used to when you deal with mental illness in your family members or loved ones. Hurt will happen. This time, in my newfound faith, I didn't want to fight anymore – but I also didn't want to keep getting hurt. I was too battle worn for another round.

Two things happened.

First, I told my mother, "I'm done, Mom. I'm not doing this anymore," and I cut ties, causing the start of a two-year estrangement. I apologized to my sisters about my choice, knowing it complicated their lives, too. I let them know that they didn't need to make special exceptions for me during family events, but this was just where I was right now.

The second thing that happened I didn't think much of at the time, but . . . well . . . that was before my perspective changed. My husband and I were in our room, and I was hurt and upset. Actually, let me be blunt here. I was pissed. I was utterly ticked off that my mother was cruel to me, angry that I would never have an adult relationship with her, tired of hearing that I wasn't good enough – that my kids weren't either, frustrated that she didn't have any idea who I even was as she kept me frozen in her memory as a snotty teenager, and most of all, unforgiving that *she* screwed me up. (Again, I recognize that she may have felt some of these same things for me.)

In my heart and mind at the time, all of it was her fault: the way I felt about myself, the decisions I'd made (just the bad ones, mind you; I took full credit for the good ones!), and the incompleteness I often felt at not having a loving mother figure. The latter of these things was to the point that my mother's expressed affections were often considered a warning sign to my sisters and me that Mom might hurt herself; they were really just "goodbye." There was also the overwhelming and panic-inducing anxiety from judgment that I lived with every day. It was all her fault.

In this state, after I'd dumped all of my disgruntled bitterness onto my husband, I said to him, "I'm done with that one. God can have her because I give up."

And . . . I did. Believe me when I say that this was not a prayer of willful surrender. This was anger. This was bitterness. This was unforgiveness.

Over the next two years, I spent time digging into the Word and learning who God really was. I'd share a testimony. I embraced random acts of kindness and spontaneous generosity. I'd share a testimony. I'd lead others. I'd share a testimony, again. We led our children to own the true Spirit of God, one of "love first."

But the fruit of the Spirit is love, joy, peace, forbearance, kindness, goodness, faithfulness, gentleness and self-control.

Galatians 5:22-23 NIV

Meanwhile, and contradictory to God's teachings, I kept my mother in a silo, separate from the rest of my faith – like I was somehow excused from not expressing love in this case. After all, she was the one who kept me from God and He didn't want that, did He? Plus, the love I did give felt wasted. I wanted better for her than she wanted for herself. She didn't want to do the work needed to be mentally healthy and emotionally well, so why should I?

After a couple of years, guilt got the best of me and I restarted our relationship again. I thought it was forgiveness. I was wrong. Our relationship became one of obligation. *'What's been keeping you busy? How's the weather, there? Listen to a short list of activities my children do. I still have my job and my husband has his. We will see one another at the next obligatory family engagement, but probably not occurring on the actual holiday, because I don't make you a real priority in my life.. 'Luv ya'! Bye until next time.'*

The thing is, God doesn't ask us to oblige one another; He asks us to *love*. There is no gray area, but I was covered in gray sludge. I was wrong every single time I ever thought I "forgave" a blowup. I didn't even understand what that word meant. Still, it's easy to float around in obligation when you don't know that's where you are. I lived there for seven years.

Then, we had to come together. It was a time in our family when we had no choice but to be on the same team to deal with something real. People think coming together in families happens for two mandatory reasons: funerals and weddings, with the latter being much preferred. I beg to differ on this myth. Each of those events, while pivotal, are just that – events. Events come and go quickly. They make picture books or memories, but they aren't our lives. We don't *live* in events. Rather, events take us out of daily life for a moment of reflection – sometimes difficult or tragic – or celebration, however fleeting. Events are pause buttons on life, not life, itself. True togetherness happens, not in events, but in seasons; when somebody is ill and needs a support system, in the time spent to heal from a tragedy, when we work together to positively influence a child's upbringing, when work, play, and life overlap, and during renovation or recovery projects of persons or places.

True togetherness happens, not in events, but in seasons.

In my family's case, we had to come together to care for somebody who had fallen on hard times and it meant we couldn't just talk about the weather. We needed to get real and we needed to be on the same team. Sure enough, not long after we stopped skimming on the surface with one another, I got hurt again. I didn't fight back, but I felt hopeless, and in the moment, chose cold obligation over love, allowing my mom to walk away in her own anger.

LET ME TAKE A MOMENT TO BREAK THE FOURTH WALL IN A WRITER'S ASIDE. I'M ABOUT TO SHARE A QUOTE THAT SOMEBODY IS GOING TO THINK BELONGS TO EINSTEIN (AS I USED TO BELIEVE), AND A FEW PEOPLE CREDIT TO BEN FRANKLIN OR MARK TWAIN. IT DOESN'T BELONG TO ANY OF THOSE MEN. IT FIRST APPEARED IN A PAMPHLET FOR NARCOTICS ANONYMOUS IN 1981 AS A GUIDE FOR ADDICTS TO BREAK THEIR ROUTINES. ALRIGHT, ASIDE OVER, BECAUSE I DO HAVE A POINT IN THIS STORY WHERE THIS PARTICULAR QUOTE FITS.

"The definition of insanity is doing the same thing over and over and expecting a different result."

It was the day before Easter and two days after the latest fight.

Something is lost when you don't have a mother, that ultimate nurturer and unconditional cheerleader in your life. I have friends who have lost this person in their lives due to illness, accident, or dementia that has caused them to forget who they are. I know those who have lost mothers to imprisonment or abandonment. Me? I had a mother who was healthy, free, and here, so what was my excuse? We didn't always get along? That wasn't good enough anymore.

"I choose forgiveness," I said to myself that morning. I said it out loud so that I could hear it, as well as speak it.

"Mom," I called her on the phone, "Why don't you come to church with us tomorrow for Easter."

I wasn't hopping onto our family's famous brush it under the rug bandwagon. This wasn't about defending myself. I was just ready to try something different in the hope of different results.

Over the next couple of months, "I choose forgiveness," was a daily mantra. I wouldn't be surprised if my mom had a similar philosophy, but – as for me – I'd start each day thinking about how to show kindness to this woman with whom I'd had decades of tension. Sometimes, I'd ask if we could go to coffee or to a community event. I kept inviting her to our church, too. I knew that our church wasn't the kind she'd struggled with in the past. "Come As You Are," is our code. Some traditional churches can feed a soul for those who need ritual. As someone from an unbelieving background, though, that wasn't for me; I assumed it wasn't for her, either.

When one of my sisters asked what this new phase was all about, I told her, "I'm trying to build a friendship with Mom. I'm being intentional about it. I'm spending time with her and having genuine conversations."

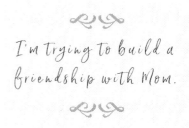

I'm trying to build a friendship with Mom.

I simultaneously was breaking down a silo and lifting up the person I'd put inside of it. The earlier meant that I had to stop denying that this relationship, and whether or not it was truly based in love, was affecting my whole life. The latter meant that I had to give time and energy to building this broken piece of my life. And, through it all, church became a routine. I assumed my mom just liked the feel-good messages, the supportive community, and the music. Not that those things aren't wonderful, but I wasn't sure she actually knew why those things existed. It wasn't because I'd surrounded myself with *good* people, but because my community was comprised of *faithful* people. It was the Spirit that made them whole and loving. Nonetheless, she had been a lifelong learner and she absorbed knowledge. She began reading her own Bible, one she'd gotten from the church, and even sharing her understanding of it with me and other family members. I never asked about this faith walk she appeared to be on. I didn't want to influence it or affect it. It was her journey; not mine.

While my mom and I were busy becoming friends, I was facilitating another class in my church. One of the teaching sessions culminates with the different leaders sharing their testimonies. I didn't want to tell mine. I usually had no problem with it. As a writer and speaker, this wasn't an area where I typically struggled. This day, though, I didn't know what I would say or how. When it came time, I told part of my story, the part that was all of my ugly – owning it – not how I got there or how I got out, just me. The second half was to come later, but I just *forgot*. In six years of being a leader in the course, that had never happened. I didn't even realize it until later. What I didn't know then was that God was changing my story. He stopped me from sharing because that old tale was no longer mine to tell.

Friendship with Mom became a reality. It's something I never dreamed of, but I truly enjoyed my time with her. After all, we did have those common interests and tastes. I began to see a change in my mother. Occasionally, she still said things that, in the past, would have hurt, but the sting wasn't in them. Once, she mentioned how she now understood

I had been witnessing a transformation in her heart.

my routine better and why I didn't have time to keep a house as organized as she did. I had to laugh to myself. Before we started to build an adult friendship, I would have felt judged and hurt that she was insulting my housekeeping. It's what she would have been doing, to be honest, but things were different now. I can't explain it, but I could feel it. I had been witnessing a transformation in her heart. What she was really saying was that she was finally seeing the life I live . . . maybe for the first time. I could tell she was trying very hard to connect to me but was just as lost about how to communicate with me as I was with her. I could tell she wanted to be well and she wanted her relationships to be healthy, too. I wanted to know this person more.

These little brushes with our new reality came more and more often, and I started to have something I had never experienced with my mom before: trust. It was trust that allowed me to invite her to one of my inner-sanctums. I was working with a group of women to study and write devotions on the Bible. This was one of our group meetings and, impulsively, I decided to bring her along. I wasn't sure how she'd feel with this group of openly faithful women, women who knew beyond a doubt that God was real; the God I'd grown up hearing was fairy tale.

She came.

At the start of the evening, the group spent some time sharing how they felt about different grief stages before we dug into Bible verses about the same. That's when my mom stepped up to the front of the room.

"I'm in a lot of pain," she said. "I was looking things up when I learned what this group was going to be about, and one of the things that hit me was Psalm 10:1 'Why, Lord, do you stand far off? Why do you hide yourself in times of trouble?'"

"My daughter knows that I had a very abusive childhood," she went on, "but I was raised in a very religious home. I gave up on God for many years. I went through depression, tried to take my life by turning the car on in the garage. That's where the police broke in and found me, grateful that I hadn't caused my own brain damage. This was because of my past with my father, and then my first husband."

Mom went on to talk about her second husband, my dad, and his ability to handle her PTSD, her nightmares, and her pain. Her strength and survival was in him, this real person, not some supernatural being.

The surreal thing for me to hear coming from my mom's mouth was, "My life started to change when I realized that God doesn't work on human time, He works on His time." She described her current season as one in which her daughter, *I*, started working with her to bring her back to God. "And then I realized," she choked up while saying, "He's always been here. He was in my husband. He's in my daughter. God – Jesus – is gradually getting me to a place of hope."

This was the first time I'd ever heard these things from my mother. I knew of her violent raising. Those were stories I'd heard about from a very young age, myself. But, to own her depression? Admit why she'd abandoned God? This was new. And hope? It was only a couple of years earlier that she had shared she didn't believe true joy existed, only survival, being productive, and having contentment with one's situation.

As a group, we worked to write about God's healing, and I gained even more insight into my mom when I was able to read her writing:

> *"God was included in my upbringing, but he never intervened to stop my abusive father. He, in fact, had years to do so. This gave rise to the thought, the idea, the almost certainty . . . that God had abandoned me. I would not raise my children with God's influence only to have that faith shattered."*

My mom was going through a transformation, but so was I.

Something broke in me that day. Don't feel bad. It was supposed to break.

Something broke in me that day. Don't feel bad. It was supposed to break. Without the *break*, how do you get *through*? In my years of leading in ministry, I had remained stuck on transformation day. I was stuck on the day of new life. That's just the beginning. I had been sitting at the starting line of my faith walk for nearly a decade.

When I heard my mom that day, I realized all the people to whom I'd shown compassion and love in my life . . . never to her. Not really. I'd had years of showing obligatory commitment as her daughter, or pity because of the circumstances of her upbringing and the lifelong mental anguish it stamped on her soul. But those things are not love. (No gray area, remember?) What's worse is that I'd been sharing a testimony that reflected a new me, despite my history of verbal damages (or the choices *I MADE* as a result of them). I allowed undeserved awe for who I'd become since my ugly character days while giving none of the same to my mother.

My moment of genuine humility was in realizing that most of my adult life had been affected by my relationship with my mother. (While emotionally messy, it was a relationship that was physically safe. Primarily, we had lifestyle or communication disagreements.) Yet I was long-exhausted by my mom being affected by *her* dad, a person who caused physical pain and tormented abuses in her life. He'd been gone for so long; I was angry he could still hold so much space in her life, as well as in every action or word she had. At the same time, here she was occupying more space in my mind and heart than ever! In that moment, I moved to my mom's side of the penny. She *had* been given tails, after all. Compassion filled my soul.

'Come on over, Mom. Check out life on the Heads' side of things.'

True forgiveness entered my heart that day, along with several realizations that highlighted what might have been my first real breakthrough since my baptism:

I surrendered Mom to God, long ago.
I chose forgiveness.
God is still writing my story.

As I go into my next decade as a Christian, I'm sure that God is looking down, seeing me take those first baby steps out of the pool into which I dove. I thought I was already a long way past the baptismal of my faith journey. It turns out my body has still been dripping all these years. Now that I've washed the water from my eyes, they are clean and clear. I see the road before me: it is honest, humbling, and Holy. *'Let's go, Mom.'*

ANGIE RIEMER is a wife of twenty-one years and mother of two. She lives in Waukesha, Wisconsin and loves the downtown vibes that the city emits. She's a former children's pastor and is also the daughter and the granddaughter of children's pastors. The desire to point people to Jesus runs deep in her family history. After facing many struggles and trials in her life, with God's help, she has managed to come through happy and healthier than she's ever been. Her passion in life is turning something old, broken and unwanted into something beautiful, desirable, and useful – just like God has done with her life.

Breakthrough

10

DEFIANT DAUGHTER

Angie Riemer

We've all seen the stereotypical teenage movies in which one character is completely two-faced, causing an aftermath of pain and anger wherever she goes. The character is often kind and gentle when with a group of friends, but the second one of them walks away, it's a different story. She tends to badmouth them and tear them apart for anything as simple as what they say, all the way up to who they are as a person. Or, the character is super sweet . . . unless you cross them and then they go out of their way to make your life a living nightmare. I'm sure that many of you know someone like this and may have even been hurt by one of them.

Well, I was that girl.

My abusive two-faced nature was not just reserved for high school I carried it with me through adulthood. I didn't behave this way because I was born mean and nasty. I behaved this way because of abuse I had sustained. Through a turn of events, I made the choice to humble myself before God and He did an amazing work in my life! He has turned my pain into passion. Because I walked through such a painful journey, I am now passionate about helping people who are facing the same struggles that I did. I offer my life as proof that, with God, ALL things are possible . . . as long as you allow him to be involved. It's important for us to remember that "hurting people, hurt people." There may occasionally be a medical reason, like a personality disorder or mental illness, that could cause a person to behave in such a hurtful manner. I've found that, the majority of the time, negative behavior like what I exhibited stems from pain. I urge you to have compassion on those that are unkind to you and pray for them. You have no way of knowing what kind of journey they have been on and their behavior may be directed toward you, but often has nothing to do with you at all.

I was not always mean with abusive tendencies; when I was a little girl I had a very happy home life. My parents were children's pastors and did a beautiful job of introducing me to Jesus in a way that made him come alive. I used to take any chance I got to tell others about Jesus because I saw him as my best friend and wanted everyone to meet him. Even though I had an amazing home life, the enemy did everything that he could to extinguish the light and happiness that I carried within me.

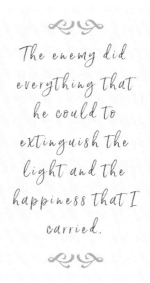

The enemy did everything that he could to extinguish the light and the happiness that I carried.

When I was five years old, my parents were ministering at a church that was led by an Army Veteran, Phil. He was an amazing guy on the surface, but was suffering from anger issues that were most likely caused from PTSD. His daughter Sarah and I had become quite close and sleepovers had become a regular thing. During the last sleepover that I'd have at their house, Sarah and I were asked to clean up our toys, so that we could leave and head to the church to meet my parents. We started to clean but, being typical kids, we got distracted and started playing again. Pastor Phil came back in a short time later to check on us and noticed that we had still not cleaned up.

He went ballistic.

He grabbed the nearest object that he could find and started to beat me and Sarah with it for not obeying his orders. I managed to get away and hid behind an overstuffed chair in their living room and cried as quietly as I could so that he couldn't hear me. I remember hearing Sarah scream as he continued to repetitively hit her, but—just as quickly as it began—his anger subsided. He came to find me in the living room and asked me to go back to clean up so that we could move on with our day. I obeyed without hesitation because I was so terrified. Ultimately, I came out of that experience with just a few bruises, but that day left an emotional scar that I would carry with me for a very long time. I learned that people are not always what they seem and, in my childlike reasoning, *I developed the belief that you can't trust your pastor.*

My parents resigned from that organization and it took us all time to heal after that occurrence. Our family started to attend a different church that we grew to love very much. At that church, we had all become very close with Karen. She was so funny and caring. My brother and I loved her so much that we called her our adopted aunt.

One thing that my brother especially loved about Karen is that she was tough. She was a Military Police Officer who had been deployed overseas and I remember how fun it was to receive mail from her and hear about her adventures. After she discharged from the Army, she lived with us for a while as she transitioned back into civilian life.

She had been sexually abused by several men in her life and family. She hated men. My mom, knowing she was broken, wanted to help her. But as she lived with us we would begin to see her true colors. Karen developed an unhealthy attachment to my mother and became very possessive of her time and attention.

One evening my brother and I were arguing, as most siblings do, and my mom started to cry. She couldn't deal with the tension in the house from our strife and the unhealthy and abusive friendship with Karen.

At seeing this, Karen became infuriated: "How dare we make her best friend cry!"

She picked my little brother up by his collar and slammed him against the wall, knocking the air out of him. He slid down the wall and onto the floor, limp but alive. When Karen saw him lying there, she became afraid at what she had done; you could tell by the look of horror she was wearing. She immediately got in my face and threatened that if I ever told my dad what I had just seen that she would use her gun to kill me and my family and that I would be the last to go, so that I could hear their screams and know that it was my mouth that had gotten them killed. I didn't sleep well for days after that had happened and, out of fear, kept quiet. Mom could no longer keep silent, though, especially now that us kids were involved. She ended up having a long conversation with my dad explaining everything that had been going on. Although he is a good Christian man, hearing that his family had been so badly treated made him very angry. He proceeded to move all of her belongings out of our house and onto our front lawn. When she returned from work that day he made sure that she understood that, after she collected her things, she was never to show her face around any of us again. She moved out and we never heard from her again.

Although she was out of our lives, I was still afraid.

Although she was out of our lives I was still afraid . . . all the time. I'd see a car like Karen's and start crying, thinking she had followed us and that it would start all over again. I'd see someone who looked like her and thinking it was her would get very angry or fall apart. It messed with me for a long time. It was *my* PTSD. I learned to distrust women and, after a second veteran had hurt us, I also distrusted anyone from the military.

Still to this day, I have not had any close relationships with women. The idea of a 'best friend' and the vulnerability that comes with that type of relationship still does not sit well with me.

That event left a scar that would take me most of my life to get rid of. The events that transpired with Karen added to the belief that began with my previous experience with Pastor Phil. I strongly mistrusted everyone, believing that people weren't ever who they seemed to be and you couldn't even trust your "best friend." Karen's actions planted a deep root of anger in my life. I felt powerless while the abuse was taking place, so I began to mentally envision myself getting even with Karen for what she did to my mother and my family. The things that I visualized myself doing to Karen in revenge were actually therapeutic. Not only were these imaginations preventing her from hurting anyone else, they were the only way that I could see justice being served. They were comforting, but very unhealthy. After allowing this practice to take place for so long, the anger began to consume me, and I became a very abrasive and unhappy individual because of it.

It always took me a while before I would allow anyone to get close to me because I wanted to analyze them first to make sure I wasn't being fooled again. Despite the fact that my intentions were good, I was constantly trying to protect myself and those that I loved which often caused unnecessary conflict and stress. Somehow in the midst of everything I developed a nasty habit of hurting those around me. The hurt that I caused was not usually intentional, but I always expected people to hurt me. So why not beat them to the punch?

> *That event left a scar that would take me most of my life to get rid of.*

I carried this unhealthy view with me into high school. I was never happy and was even angry in my sleep. I would wake up with my fists clenched leaving indentions in the palms of my hand from my finger nails. I didn't care; I actually liked my new tough persona; it kept me safe. I started to dress all in dark colors and wore dark lipstick and thick eyeliner. When coupled with my pale complexion I was slightly reminiscent of Marilyn Manson. Most people at school completely avoided me, which is exactly what I wanted. Those that didn't only knew fractions of who I really was because I was afraid of close connections. The only thing that truly brought me joy was when I was causing others pain by verbally cutting them down or by mildly causing physical harm. I was an absolute mess!

My newly acquired attitude began to affect everything and everyone in my life. It also began to affect my health. I had constant stomach aches all of the time and nothing I did gave me any relief. I'd seen multiple doctors trying to figure out the cause of my discomfort. It was eventually determined that stress was the main source of my pain. The only thing doctors could do was to suggest that I reduce the number of stressors in my life in order to alleviate the pain. This was so much easier said than done. I was in a constant state of tension and I didn't know how to fix it. There was no one that could help me and the stomach pain seemed to get more severe on a daily basis. This went on for a several years. I was told by numerous doctors that there was nothing that could be done and a couple of them told me that this was all in my head. I almost started to believe them, until I actually started to develop symptoms that would prove to them that this pain was real. I began to pass blood and mucus in my stool on top of the pain. I went to see a GI specialist and, after doing a colonoscopy, it was discovered that I had Crohn's disease.

I was in a constant state of tension and I didn't know how to fix it.

It turns out that doctors had been partially right all along. With Inflammatory Bowel Disease (Crohn's, Colitis, and even Irritable Bowel Syndrome), one of the main triggers is stress. After receiving my diagnosis, "How's your stress level?" would be the first question I was asked every time I went to the doctor. The burning stabbing stomach aches and constant trips to the bathroom that are embodied by this disease are aggravated every time a stressor is introduced into your environment. Because I had chosen to welcome the stress of hatred and fear in to my life on a daily basis I was basically stuck. However, no matter how severe the pain had gotten, or how full of hatred I'd become, I still managed to hold on to my childhood love for Jesus and believed that he would heal me.

When I was very young I had several life altering experiences that would cultivate my faith in God. The first experience took place when I was just fifteen-months old. One evening as my mom was cooking dinner I managed to squeeze through a baby gate into our tiny little kitchen. Mom didn't realize that I was at her feet and as she turned to drain a pot of boiling water in the sink, she stumbled spilling the water over my tiny body. I was taken to the Emergency Room and then to a burn center. While doctors were able to perform some skin grafting, because of my size and the amount of skin that had been burned they were not able to surgically treat all of the areas affected. Without skin grafting much of my body was going to be permanently scarred. My parents were told that nothing more could be done. As I lay in my hospital bed wrapped in bandages, my father laid hands on me and prayed believing that God would heal me. When the bandages were removed, the area on my chest that received skin grafts was still recovering, but all other areas that had been affected by the burns were completely healed.

Not long after the burning incident, I was a very sick two-and-a half year old. I had allergies to everything: pets, grass, chocolate, poultry proteins, you name it. When the allergist tested me, I was found to be allergic to every single thing that they looked for. I was very sick and completely housebound.

"This is *not* how Jesus wants you to live," my dad said. "Do you want to go out and play . . . eat what you want . . . not be sick all the time?"

Of course that's what I wanted! Most of all, being a toddler, I just wanted to have the chocolate covered cookies they gave out for snack time in my church's nursery. My dad prayed over me a second time and God once again healed me. All of the allergies were gone. One of my earliest memories is being back in the nursery at church and not having to sit apart from the other kids during snack time.

My Jesus healed me.

"My Jesus healed me," I said and I was excited to enjoy my first chocolate covered cookie without an anaphylactic response.

Healing was real for me, but my early childhood incidents led to a weakened immune system that, combined with stress of the abuses in my life, led to Crohn's disease having a window of entry into my life.

I underwent treatment for over a year after the initial diagnosis with no luck. My health began to deteriorate so severely that, at age twenty, I weighed just seventy-nine pounds and had to be hospitalized because I was too weak to stand without assistance. The disease had spread rapidly and had begun to destroy the skin and tissue on my rear end. I refused to eat because the outcome was too incredibly painful, so they hooked me up to a feeding tube to sustain me and prevent me from losing more weight. I started violently throwing up. Let me tell you that vomiting while sporting a feeding tube is its own special kind of torture. It's like drowning in vomit. I could no longer breathe out of my nose, so doctors had no other choice than to remove the feeding tube. I was rapidly getting worse.

While being treated, I had a seizure and was rushed down for an MRI to see what had caused it. I had a tumor the size of a gumball near the center of my brain and was immediately scheduled for brain surgery.

While the tumor was not cancerous, I was so weak and had so much blood loss during surgery, that doctors told my family I realistically only had about three months to live. My family was silent after that, we had all just been hit by a freight train of bad news and no one knew how to react. That night as my mom drove home from the hospital, she was sobbing uncontrollably. Through her tears, she happened to glance up and see that there was a beautiful and bright full moon in the sky.

As she looked at it, God spoke to her. "Isn't it beautiful when you see the whole picture?"

My mom thought of the "whole" picture . . . miraculously healed skin where grafts were not done . . . a chocolate-covered toddler who was once allergic to everything . . . a tumor that could have been cancerous but wasn't. Healing *was* real for today and real for me. Her tears of sorrow quickly turned to tears of joy at hearing this because, although she could not see how I could possibly recover, in that moment she knew that I was going to live.

I really could not see how God was going to work this out. The situation seemed hopeless. Since doctors were no longer able to help me, I made the choice to check out of the hospital and go home, but within a couple of days my condition went from bad to worse and my family had to call an ambulance to take me to the emergency room. During the ambulance ride, I asked the paramedics to take me to a different hospital than the one that I was recently discharged from. I was hoping a new set of eyes would turn my situation around. Once there, the on-call doctor was actually a colon and rectal surgeon. After examining me, he agreed with my initial doctor's decision that surgery was too risky to perform, but without it I *would* die. He said that he was willing to perform the surgery that

I needed to save my life as long as I understood how dangerous it was.

The operation was long, but I came out of it. I was in more pain than I had ever been in but found hope in that pain because I thought that this time it was only temporary. It wasn't. Surgery after surgery was performed, always fixing something that was broken. I was upset that no one could figure out how to fix this. This process repeated over and over again for two years. The wounds of my colon and rectum did eventually heal but the other issues wouldn't go away. The pain was more severe than ever. I had 6 inches of my colon dangling out of my stomach into my colostomy bag and during an examination it was discovered that had actually become gangrenous. They scheduled me for yet another surgery to correct this newly acquired issue but this time they decided to remove my entire colon.

I was hopeless.

I was so annoyed and discouraged at this point and didn't understand why this was happening to me. My mom had a word from God that I was going to be okay, so why was I still sick? I mean, I loved and served God with all my heart. I was constantly quoting scripture, praying, and was doing everything right, so why was everything always going so wrong? I cried out to God and asked for help. And like the good father that he is he answered almost immediately in a very gentle but firm and loving way.

> I loved and served God....so why was everything always going so wrong?

A member of my church asked if he could come pray with me. I was more than happy to accept all prayers that I could get so I agreed. As he began lay his hand on my forehead to pray, he quickly pulled it back and said something that would change my life.

He said, "I don't understand this, but I know you will, I can't pray for you just yet. God wants me to tell you something first....If you don't let this go, it *will* be the death of you."

I started sobbing the instant that he said that because I knew exactly what he meant.

As I mentioned, I was harboring some full-fledged hatred and unforgiveness toward several people and it consumed me, However I had grown up in the church and *knew* that this behavior was wrong. The whole time that I was experiencing all of my health issues, I'd quote scriptures and pray . . . and then a song would come on the radio that would make me think of either Phil, Karen or somebody else who had hurt me and I would literally grit my teeth with anger. I would thank Jesus for his healing power . . . and then get stuck in traffic and start imagining how great it would be if the reason that there was a traffic jam was because one of those people had gotten in a car accident and had died a slow and painful death. I would sing praises to God for saving my life . . . and moments later would secretly be wishing that one of my abusers would be losing theirs. I had more than distrust; I had actual hate-filled anger toward women, military persons, pastors, and anybody else I thought could possibly hurt me.

This was not a healthy place to be at all! The Bible says that you cannot serve two masters (Matthew 6:24), and at that point in my life, even though I did love God, I was a servant to hatred.

Essentially what I was saying with my behavior was, *'God I love You, but I don't like the way that You want me to do things because it's too hard. So I am going to hate my enemies instead of loving them because it's easier. I'm going to take judgment into my own hands instead of trusting You to handle it. I'm going to speak death over these individuals rather than being Jesus to them and showing them how to truly live. I love You, God, but I think that I can handle this better than You can.'*

I was being outright defiant! I knowingly and willingly was disobeying God and, even though I really did love him, he was no longer my Master. My true masters were hatred, fear, resentment, and anger. These masters dictated how I behaved on a daily basis and how I treated everyone I came into contact with. I willingly obeyed them because it made me feel better emotionally (I thought). And because I chose to serve them instead of God, it opened the door for spiritual and even physical torment. God will not hear us if we allow hate to live in our hearts (Mark 11:25-26) because darkness is not allowed where there is light.

Loving and serving God is not about what feels good and what coddles our emotions. It's about doing what's right and choosing to love the unlovable. I prayed and asked God for forgiveness. From that day on, I made the choice to forgive my abusers. It sounds easy, right? Nope; it's one of the hardest battles I have had to fight.

Loving and serving God is not about what feels good and what coddles our emotions.

Whenever I'd start thinking about what my abusers had done to me or my family I would ask myself this question: "What happened to *them* to make them treat people that way?" and then I would pray for them.

I'm not going to lie, the last thing that I wanted to do for these people was pray for them. The first time that I prayed was for Karen. She was the one who had hurt me the most, so that's where I started. I was shaking and crying because it went against every fiber of my being. In my mind, they were deserving of my hatred and not my prayers, but—when I made it a habit to pray for them every day—my whole thought process toward all people changed, not just to those who had wronged me. Changing my thinking began to soften me and my life began to change. My health began to drastically improve because I wasn't flooding my body with toxic stress hormones on a daily basis.

Today I am proud to say that I have been completely healed from Crohn's disease. A lot of you are probably reading that in disbelief because, according to medical science, Crohn's is incurable. But I mean what I say: I am **healed** from Crohn's. I haven't had a single symptom and have been off of all Crohn's medications for more than ten years. I can eat anything that I want with absolutely no stomach aches or flair ups. I still go to see my gastroenterologist doctor once a year and, every time he sees me, he shakes his head in disbelief.

I not only have been healed from Crohn's disease, my bitter and resentful heart has healed as well. I have learned to approach people with love rather than being two faced and spiteful.

I went from hatred to prayer.

I went from defiant child to daughter of God.

I went from near death to completely healed.

It truly is beautiful now that I can see the whole picture!

VICTORIA DRECKMAN is a fitness instructor, author, and speaker. Her desire is to mentor and encourage women in their daily walk as they tackle life's F-words - Faith Family Fitness Food. Her willingness to show truth, authenticity, and raw vulnerability through her writing speaks to the hurt woman in all of us. She resides in Delafield, Wisconsin with her husband and two of her three children. You can follow her on Facebook at **https://www.facebook.com/LiveVictoryUs/** *"We must be willing to get rid of the life we've planned, so as to have the life that is waiting for us." Joseph Campbell (1904-1987)*

Breakthrough

II

I'm Staying With You

Victoria Dreckman

ctober 21, 2000

I approached the decorative concrete walkway leading to the beautifully colored and fragrant rose garden. I could see everyone seated in their chairs, facing the gazebo where my handsome groom and I would soon exchange vows. This was it. We had talked about this day, planned for it, and now it was finally here. Our wedding party was small, two people, since this was my second wedding and we both wanted something simple and quaint. My thoughts were lost in how I knew this marriage was going to go the distance.

I just knew it.

The wedding coordinator instructed us to begin walking down the quaint pathway as the harpist and violinist began playing *The Bells Processional*. My stomach was in knots, and my hands shook holding my bouquet of three dozen white and sterling silver roses as I watched my future sister-in-law proceed down the path. Next in the procession was my five-year-old daughter, Taylor. She looked

157

adorable holding her delicate mini bouquet with her hair in a sweet little up-do.

It was my turn.

I took a deep breath as I took my first step down the aisle to meet my husband-to-be.

I can't tell you much about what happened after that, because it was all a blur. I do remember crying most of the way through my vows because I was so happy to have found this man. He tolerated many challenging and troubling situations involving my ex-husband and had also taken on the responsibility of step-dad without even blinking an eye.

Soon after the wedding, life carried on as usual. We filled our lives with Taylor's soccer games, yard work, and enjoying the company of our friends. We tried attending church here and there, but never made it a priority. Unfortunately, we did what a lot of newlyweds do; we just stopped going.

Summer 2002...

My husband was offered a job with a large international retail chain and we were all excited about this opportunity. It was the perfect chance to advance his career to new heights. However, it meant moving out-of-state. Our excitement was short-lived, though, as my ex-husband would not allow me to move out-of-state with Taylor. So began the downward spiral in my marriage. My husband's disappointment and stress levels increased as our intimacy and communication decreased.

During this tumultuous time, I really felt the pull on my heart to get our family back to church, especially after the birth of our daughter, Zoe. My neighbors across the street regularly attended a Lutheran church, and since I had grown up Lutheran, I decided to check it out. I liked the pastors and the deacon, and Taylor seemed to like it for the most part. We decided to join. At that time, new members would have their picture taken as a family – it would be put into a church directory. This particular directory listed where each spouse worked.

Upon distribution of this directory, my husband received several calls at work from people who were members of the church (and didn't even have relationship with Dan) inquiring about jobs. It was his perfect excuse. He wanted his Sundays back and this inappropriate intrusion on his professional life served as a legitimate reason to say he was done with the church. At that moment, he made up his mind that he wasn't going to church with us anymore. He was done. That broke my heart.

I struggled as a mom of a two-year-old and my pre-teen, Taylor. She, like many teenagers, didn't want the responsibilities of growing up like chipping in at home, helping to take care of her younger sister, and being a part of the family.

In addition, I was often at home by myself from early in the morning until late in the evening. I had friends that I would connect with during the day to meet for coffee or playdates with the kids, and – in the evenings – I'd attend a cardio kickboxing class to let out all of my frustrations. One evening after class, my instructor and friend noticed I was exerting way more energy than usual. I confided in her what we were experiencing with Taylor . . . a completely defiant behavior. She suggested I come to a Boundaries for Kids book study at her church.

I had no idea this church would be the catalyst for a spiritual awakening in my life. I attended the first service with such trepidation as I watched the women around me pray, sing, and even weep openly with arms raised high. I was uncomfortable at first,

I had no idea this church would be the catalyst for a spiritual awakening in my life.

159

constantly looking around to see if anyone was staring at me, as if they somehow knew I was a "Lutheran." However, as Pastor Patsy spoke, I felt this overwhelming emotion well up inside of me. I felt the tears flow from my eyes and I couldn't stop them. A warmth, like wrapping yourself in a fuzzy, just-out-of-the-drier blanket enveloped me from the top of my head all the way to my toes. I felt a compassion within that I had never experienced before as I stood in awe. I realized Jesus was here with me. I had the head knowledge of this for more than thirty years, but this was an affair of the heart.

From that moment forward, I pursued everything I could get my hot little hands on to learn more, know more, and experience more of Jesus.

I was all in!

The scriptures suddenly came alive to me as I studied. There was a depth and meaning in the Bible that I had never noticed before. At the same time, my husband and I grew further apart. There wasn't anything terrible happening either…just the routines of the day. He'd go to work, I'd do my thing with the kids, and we would meet in the bedroom at night. That was just married life, so I thought.

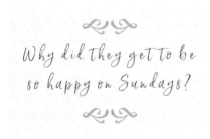

Why did they get to be so happy on Sundays?

My daughters and I started attending this new church regularly. I'd drop them off in children's church and then find a seat in the worship center. I sat down and enviously began perusing the room of families and couples. Why did they get to be together on Sundays? More importantly, why couldn't I have my husband here with me? I'd watch the couple in front of me as the husband extended his arm around the back of the chair and tenderly rubbed his wife's shoulders. To my far left was the older woman who saved her husband a seat while he ushered. He'd awkwardly bend over to kiss his wife before sitting down. There was a family next to me with the daddy sweetly rocking his toddler as she drifted off to sleep, her adorable little head resting on his shoulder.

'This is not fair!' I'd scream in my head, *'I want that!'*

About that time, I started attending a prayer circle with a group of ladies I had not yet met from my church. This was an amazing group of women with whom I have since formed a forever bond. We set aside one morning a week to pray for our husbands. Let me be clear; this was not a gripe and moan session about the things we didn't like about our husbands. This was a group of women, going through some really tough stuff, and encouraging each other through the Word of God (Bible) and prayer.

There is great value in seeking advice from more seasoned Christian women. They've been there, done that, and can point you to help:

> *"Wives, in the same way submit yourselves to your own husbands so that, if any of them do not believe the word, they may be won over without words by the behavior of their wives, when they see the purity and reverence of your lives."*
>
> *◈ 1 Peter 3:1-2 NIV*

As a wife, I was to be good to my husband, respectful, and responsive to his needs, in spite of the fact that he was far from the Lord. They encouraged me to stay true to the scriptures because my husband could be won over to the Lord by the gentle quiet spirit within me.

Just as I would start to believe that, and really walk it out, I'd go to book study group and hear a woman give testimony that, "she's been believing God for twenty years that her husband will come to the Lord."

Every time I'd hear a similar story this voice would rise up inside of me and scream, "No! I am not waiting twenty years!"

October 2006...

"My husband is going to get saved today."

At least that is what I said almost every day when I woke up. Word of warning, as your faith and convictions increase, so do the attacks of the enemy. Around this same time, my husband encountered difficulties at his job and we suffered some major financial blows. Major. One evening he was in a tirade about it all as I quietly sat and listened to him unload his frustrations. I became an expert at, "listen but don't speak."

This particular day, he kept staring me down as he went on and on, until he finally asked, "Why aren't you getting angry? These people are trying to take us out! Doesn't this make you upset?!"

I looked at him briefly before responding, "You know, I'm not upset or angry. I know the Lord is going to take care of this, too."

That might not have been the best thing to say at that particular moment, but it is what I said. Somehow, this led to a discussion about how you get to heaven.

His response, "I'm a good person. I think God sees I'm good and I go to heaven."

He wasn't going to Heaven. He had no idea that Jesus was the only way there.

My heart broke, yet again. I realized at that moment, not only was my husband not going to church, but he wasn't going to heaven. He had no idea that Jesus was the only way there.

Christmas time arrived, and we were visiting my husband's family in Wisconsin. We attended my sister-in-law's church on Christmas Eve. I was extremely excited when Dan decided to go to church with us that evening. It was during that service that the Holy Spirit spoke to my heart. I stood there, quietly praying to myself for my husband to receive Jesus.

Then, that still small voice inside of me said, "It will be soon. Not yet, but soon."

I had to stop and evaluate if that was really the Holy Spirit or just my wishful thinking. I chose to believe it was the voice of the Holy Spirit.

Two Months Later...

I decided to plan a date night with my husband. I tried everything I could to be the wife I knew I was supposed to be for him. We left the house in the frigid February rain . . . silence. Sitting at the table in the restaurant we ordered our meal . . . silence. The conversation we did have was forced and awkward. I could feel my heart sinking into my stomach by the end of dinner. The car ride home . . . more silence. I paid the babysitter and went off to bed early . . . silently.

That night, I cried out to God in my loneliness. *'Lord, I know you're there. You said you'd never leave me or forsake me. But please, you have to do something because I can't take this solitude anymore. You said you would stay with me. Stay with me in this. I don't want to have another failed marriage. Please do something.'*

I pulled the covers tightly around my neck, curled my body into a tight ball, and cried myself to sleep.

That next morning, Sunday, I awoke and lay there for a moment before asking Dan the dreaded question I asked every Sunday morning. "Do you want to go to church with us today?"

He usually responded with a quick "no." Not this morning.

"If I do, I don't want to talk about it afterwards. Not a word."

My heart leapt for joy!

Cool and collected, I responded, "Okay. No talking. No problem."

I immediately jumped out of bed to get myself ready in record time.

In the fashion of a drill sergeant, I informed the children, "Dad is going to church with us this morning. There will be no arguing, no fighting, no questions. Just get up, get your breakfast and get in the car. Have I made myself clear?" I was determined to make this the smoothest event ever.

Dan began regularly attending Sunday services with us. It was about two months after this that his nightmares began (unknown to me) and I attended a Friday night service at my church, alone. On my way home, I was overcome with the need to pray in the spirit. I've learned to be obedient to these promptings over time and went right into it. I prayed fervently and loudly. I felt as if I was demanding, rather than requesting, and I was not going to back down . . . no matter what happened. I prayed the entire ride home, until this peace came over me which was an indication that I had prayed through whatever I was being prompted to pray.

The next morning, I took the kids to see the *Veggie Tales* movie, *The Pirates Who Don't Do Anything*.

When we arrived back home, Dan was waiting for me by the counter in the kitchen, "We need to talk, in private."

Something was wrong; he never did this before, but I had no clue what was bothering him.

He led me into through the house and into the bedroom where he closed the door behind me and sat on the edge of the bed. Almost to the point of tears, he tells me, "I think I'm going crazy." That is certainly not what I expected to hear.

"Why do you think that?" I ask.

He began telling me of the chilling nightmares that consumed him every night, causing him to wake up with his heart racing and in a cold sweat. They consumed his thoughts throughout the day. For me, it was literally out of the blue. I had no idea this had been going on. I was in shock.

We had been taking baby steps to grow back toward each other through faith, but here he was really sharing something personal with me. I listened to him with a compassionate ear, wanting to solve the problem, but I really only knew one answer.

We had been taking baby steps to grow back toward each other in faith.

"I don't know what to say except, you need Jesus."

I was totally unprepared for his next statement which blew me out of the water, "Okay. How do I do that?"

It was a privilege and honor to lead my husband to the Lord Jesus that afternoon. I'd like to say that this is the happy ending to my story, but it was only a mile marker on our journey.

March 2008...

Dan was now a business owner, spending a ridiculous amount of time and effort with his partner getting their business off the ground. They were quite successful, despite it being the height of a recession at the conception of their venture. This career came with an immense amount of stress, problems, and some people that were less than respectable. His disposition was always negative, his temper short, and he was always "checked out" around the family. I had tried repeatedly to connect with him in many different ways. I'd tell him what I needed from him physically, emotionally, and sexually. Yes, ladies, sometimes you need to voice that subject too. I'm not exaggerating when I say I tried *everything* to make our marriage better. Don't get me wrong, he never raised a hand to me or emotionally or mentally abused me. He would never even think of doing that. Nonetheless, we had become roommates. I was also the

165

housekeeper, chef, and entertainment director. I desperately desired to hear, "You look beautiful" or "You are the love of my life". I yearned for him to wrap one hand around the back of my neck and the other around my waist and pull me close to him and kiss me passionately. Believe me when I say, I specifically told him, *'if you do these things: x, y, and z, you are golden and are guaranteed to get lucky.'*

His response was, "Are we really doing this? Are you serious?"

Yes. I was serious about needing our intimacy. It wasn't a joke or melodramatic. That was the moment *I* checked out.

I continued to go to church, volunteer, and attend bible study groups, but it wasn't the same. Then came Facebook. I was on my way into the grocery store when a notification popped up on my phone. It said, "You have a friend request from '*Brian.*'"

Not gonna lie, I got a little excited to see that. You see, Brian was my first true love at the age of fifteen. We kept in touch here and there over the past twenty-five plus years, but—with the invention of Facebook—it allowed us to be a bigger presence in each other's lives . . . I had just opened the door for the enemy and invited him into my life. He didn't force it open. I gave him the key.

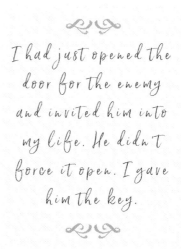

I had just opened the door for the enemy and invited him into my life. He didn't force it open. I gave him the key.

What happened next is a prime example of how the enemy deceives us. First, did you know that—once you open that door for the enemy—he will most likely deliver your every *desire*, right to your doorstep? It's true. You see, what my husband wasn't fulfilling in me, I temporarily found fulfillment for . . . through Brian. I say "temporarily" because, truth be told, the only thing that was going to fill that emptiness was Jesus.

I journaled all my deepest desires, knowing I was safe if I kept them between myself and a piece of paper. I started making up stories to appease my creative imagination. I texted Brian on a regular basis, too. Most conversations were topical . . . nothing serious. On occasion, he would mention how beautiful he thought I was from a picture on Facebook. That really spurred my ego, especially since I wasn't hearing that from my husband at the time.

At church, our women's ministry pastor gave a word of knowledge to the group of ladies. "If you are married and talking secretly to people of the opposite sex on Facebook, I'm here to tell you that you need to end that communication right now. You are creating an emotional tie to someone who is not your husband and that is a form of adultery."

My spirit was convicted but my flesh screamed, "You have no idea what I'm going through. This person makes me feel better!"

The words of James chapter 1 verse 14 were never clearer than now: "but each person is tempted when they are dragged away by their own evil desire and enticed."

In that moment, I told the Lord "I've done things your way and haven't gotten anywhere. I'm not gonna walk away from my husband, but I am done trying."

What a true Israelite moment, am I right? I'd seen God's hand touch my life in miraculous ways, yet, in the midst of my desert experience, I had forgotten how good He had been to me. I had even justified my actions by using God's own words (twisted, of course). *'After all, even King David, a man after God's heart, not only had an affair, he killed someone! I'm not that bad!'* Folks, don't do that. That was a lie straight from the pit of hell that I ate right up.

I never crossed "that" actual line, but there were lines I did cross:
   Giving personal information about my marriage to an outsider of it . . . making him a confidant.
   Allowing my imagination to run away with me . . . about another man.

Opening myself up to feelings of pride over another man's compliments (rather than recognize these things for the flaming arrows to my marriage that they were).

I thank God that He pursued me with a vengeance, or I might have been allowed to fall even deeper into my pit of sin.

April 2014...

I prepared to go to an out-of-state conference to gather my continuing education credits for my fitness certification when everything came to a crashing halt. Dan pulled me aside to talk. Over the course of that past week, I had noticed Dan had been unusually attentive to me and my needs. What came next, I did not see coming.

He approached me, "I was in the bedroom the other day and something in my head told me to look in this drawer and under those clothes. I found this."

He stood holding my journal in his hands. He read it cover to cover and was heartbroken by what he read. I did not expect what happened next.

"I don't completely blame you. After I read this, I knew in an instant all the things you wanted from me before . . . all the attention and affection things . . . I don't know why I couldn't do them before, but I can do them all now. I don't know what was stopping me, either. If you are willing to stay with me, to work things out because you want to be with me, then I promise you I will be this changed man for the rest of our lives."

Dan took ownership of his part in our brokenness, too, in that moment – the lines he crossed and vows he didn't keep.

He didn't give the attention and intimacy that I craved as his wife:

Things he'd spoken in anger, rather than letting the Holy Spirit flow out, when he felt frustration or impatience.

The adultery he had with *his* "other person" . . . his job.

We had each let one another down, and let God down, and God doesn't weigh sin; man does. In His eyes, we'd both messed up.

You would think that after Dan's words, I would jump into his arms and say "YES!" but actually, I was angry. How could he all of a sudden decide to change *now*? What about the past seven to ten years? Why should I believe him?

I stood staring blankly at him, part of me wanting to believe him, yet another part of me thinking, "Here we go again. How long will it last this time?" I told him I needed to think it over.

That night, I tried to think about what to say. I knew I didn't want our marriage to end, but I also was tired of repeating this pattern. All the Bible verses I had learned over the past fourteen years about marriage and love came rushing into my mind. *Wives respect your husbands. Husbands love your wives.* (Ephesians, Peter) *Love is patient. Love is kind. Love doesn't want what it doesn't have. Love doesn't keep a record of wrongs. Love puts up with anything, trusts God always, always looks for the best, never looks back, but keeps going to the end. To the end, forever and ever until death do us part.* (1 Corinthians)

Sunday morning, I finished getting ready for church before facing him, knowing he was awake and expected me to give him my answer.

My answer was, "I'm staying with you. I love you and know that the wonderful man I met over fourteen years ago is still in you. And if you truly can do what you *say* you are going to do, then we can trust in the Lord for the rest to line up."

We can Trust in the Lord. . . .

That morning, Dan and I both rededicated ourselves to the Lord and we haven't returned to our old selves, since. We became new creatures in Christ, born again, and we were ready to go the distance and make our marriage last . . . until death do us part.

MEET YOUR BREAKTHROUGH AUTHOR

TRACI WELDIE is high school Learning Specialist, teacher, coach, and small group leader. Traci is a co-founder of an adoption and foster care conference, Refresh, for women located in Upstate South Carolina. She has six children, two of whom are adopted, which has led to a desire to encourage and equip women who have made the decision to care for the fatherless. Traci has written with vulnerability and honesty what it has been like to adopt children with special needs. Married to her best friend for twenty-two years, Traci enjoys sitting on the back porch with Joe.

Breakthrough

12

I AM GEORGE

Traci Weldie

When we first brought him home, I was not prepared for what would happen next. George stood in the corner of the living room crying. When I tried to console him, he ran into his bedroom where he proceeded to tear off all the outer-space sheets from his bed, leaving them in a heap in the middle of the floor. He then threw all the stuffed animals that friends and family had given him as his "Welcome Home" present across the room. Then, George looked right at me with his deep brown eyes and his gorgeous brown skin as he ripped, page by page, the photobook of his new family I had created for him from a mother's love. This was not what I thought adoption would look like.

But, this is not the story of George. This is not the story of a boy who had been adopted from Ethiopia when he was six years old. Naively, I thought my life would be that story, that I would stand before you sharing the beautiful, redemptive picture of adoption. God, however, had an altogether different story in mind when He called my husband and me to adoption. God knew this momma needed to change, so this is MY story; the story of a woman learning who God really is . . . and who she really was.

I will take you back to the very first year, where my story of breakthrough began.

I remember the wood floor of the old farmhouse's office was hard, and I stared blankly at the small scratch marks my German Shepherd had made over the years by scampering through the room every time one of the kids ran into the kitchen. I had a carload of kids, and they did quite a bit of running into the kitchen, so I had several scratch marks to focus on. I rested my back against the wall, throwing my head down in defeat. Specific words jostled through my mind fighting to take dominance of my thoughts; everything from, *'I am so exhausted!'*, to *'I can't even believe how he just treated me!'* Every thought had the same purpose: pointing me toward waving the white flag.

God had spoken so clearly to me the year before, "I'm calling you to adopt."

Our family of six was on vacation in New Jersey and my husband and I were watching our children playing. We were thinking, *'we can do more.'* We challenged one another to pray about adoption and we spent the whole week trying to discern if this was our calling.

When God spoke to me, He spoke to my husband, too; it was in the midst of our time of reading scripture, praying, and focusing on the Holy Spirit. It was one of those moments where we knew without a doubt that this was right. We were on the same page, receiving the same message from God. Even when times have been hard, it's undeniable that this is what we were called to do.

Funny, I simply had no idea at the time that God was actually calling me to open my heart to brokenness, pain, and trauma; God was asking me not just to adopt a child, but to completely turn my comfortable, North-American, Christian life upside down. Now, I sat on the floor outside my son's bedroom, I the broken one, I the one with scars and bruises. I had prayed for this! I did not want to have a faith that just went through the motions and took God for granted. God answered that prayer in George.

I was that good-Christian girl; going to church, being somewhat devoted to a daily . . . well maybe a weekly, if I am being honest . . . quiet time. I now had a son who threw things across the room when he was told "no," and whined constantly when I didn't set before him another plate of macaroni and cheese (which was the only food he would eat for four months). He tore apart photographs and books, called his new siblings horrible names, and completely rejected this momma's love.

During this season, mornings began quite commonly. I would lie in bed dreading the day ahead of me, but pulling together some amount of strength to get out of bed, I would greet George with a smile and a gentle word, "Good morning."

He would shrug, not making eye contact, and walk right by me heading toward the kitchen for his beloved macaroni and cheese. I would offer him breakfast, maybe scrambled eggs or some waffles; the same things I was offering all of my children.

George would wag his finger at me and shout, "No!"

With each wag of the finger and turn of the head, it was as if George was saying, "I don't want you, Momma. I want something else right now. I do not want what you are offering me. I want something you haven't offered me."

I would stand hopeless in my kitchen yet again. *'How can I show this child how much I want to love him?'*

As I hugged and kissed the other kids going off to school, George would whine at the window as he watched the yellow school bus bound away. That whining would eventually turn into an hour-long screaming session. I would gently put my arms around him and try to move him to the couch where I would promise to read his favorite book.

Again, the wagging finger and the one English word he had mastered, "No!"

Lunch would come with more refusals followed by me just watching from the front porch as George doggedly attempted to ride a bike . . . all by himself, not letting me hold the bike steady or run alongside him.

I would cheer with joy inside my rattled mind when I saw the first glimpse of the bouncing school bus coming down the lane bringing the other kids home from school – finally I would have someone who wanted to see me and spend time with me! Shortly after, my husband would come home and I would fall into his arms for an extra-long hug. I would busy myself with making dinner, throwing in some more dirty laundry, cleaning up the kitchen, picking up toys, helping with homework, drawing baths, making lunches for the next day, and basically doing all the things moms do for their children.

Bedtime always brought out more pain. George would refuse the nighttime story on the couch with the siblings. He would turn his back on me when it was time for goodnight hugs and kisses. As I would reach for the astronaut covers to tuck him in, he would violently throw them back to the foot of the bed and close his eyes, pretending he was asleep.

Sighing heavily, I would walk up the old farmhouse stairs to tuck in my girls.

As I knelt by their bedsides to pray, I often admitted, "Girls, I simply don't have any words. I just don't understand why he continues to reject me."

After hugs and kisses, I would go back downstairs to where George and his little brother shared a bedroom. *I'm going back in to try again.* Even though my heart and mind were screaming, *'No more,'* something was constantly moving me back to pursue.

I laid my hand on George's back, said my goodnight, and broke a little more as he squirmed away from the weight of my hand. I moved over to the other twin bed where Lincoln was watching me with sad eyes. I kissed Lincoln, gave him a hug, tussled his blonde hair, and walked out of the room. Then, I sat down right outside the room, broken hearted and done.

"Lord, I just don't understand! All I want to do is love this child and spend time with him. If he would just turn to me, he would see that I'm here to be his momma, to love him forever."

The Holy Spirit works in mysterious ways in these quiet, dark moments. The Lord's gentle response came quietly, "Traci, this is how you treat me most days."

Stunned, I asked God, "Did you really just say that this is how I treat you?"

"Yes, my daughter."

I forced myself to think. This whole experience had been a huge metaphor of my relationship with God. Each morning, God wants to greet me, sing over me, love me . . . and I tend to shake my finger at him and say, "Not now. I need my coffee. That is what I need to wake up."

This whole experience had been a huge metaphor of my relationship with God

God sighs and calls out to me again, "Come sit with me now."

Then, I remember that pile of laundry that needs to be moved from the washer to the dryer before the clothes get all stinky.

"Hang on God, as soon as I finish what really needs to be done."

God patiently waits, gently calling me, "Come sit with me."

But, I have clothes to fold now, and I have to pick up those toys that Lincoln left out and I want to be sure to check Facebook to see how my friends are doing.

God calls, "Come. I just want to love you."

I reply with, "Have you seen how long our house has been on the market? Can you please sell our house? And, how about giving us a beautiful day today so we can play outside? Have you seen Harry lately? Can you please heal his cold?"

On and on my list of requests makes its way to God and I expect an answer. I expect action.

I *am* George.

I am the child whose parent is standing there simply wanting to pour out love. But, if I am honest, what God is offering me just doesn't seem appealing at the time. That is, until I need something, then God had better be there for me. God has been holding a mirror up to my face, showing me how I act, but more importantly *HOW* He loves. God has loved me with patience, abandon, passion, and relentless pursuit! Moreover, most days, I just simply miss that amazing love because it is not what I want.

Sitting on the floor, I remembered an email from a friend that had come in a few days early. "Read Hosea," was all she said.

I decided, "Why not start reading it now? I really have nothing to lose at this point."

I walked into the living room where Joe was reclining on the couch watching baseball. He smiled at me and held my hand for a bit as I walked by him to reach the bookshelf. There, my eye caught my bright blue *Message.* After humming my "Books of the Old Testament" song in my head, I found Hosea and started reading the introduction back at my spot on the hardwood floor outside the boys' bedroom. I stopped cold at this sentence: "God loves us in just this way – goes after us at our worst, keeps after us until he gets us, and makes lovers of men and women who know nothing of real love."

I threw my head back and just let that message truth sink in. God chases us down even when we are selfishly wagging our finger at him. God's desire to love us is unfathomable to my human mind, and I truly know nothing about love until I understand the depth and the height and the vastness of His love for me.

So many thoughts were racing through my mind: *'How could I have missed this understanding of God's love and pursuit of us, after all, I was one of those good Christian girls? I had gone to church, led Bible studies . . . heck, I even adopted a child because I was that good Christian girl.'*

But, where was my heart? Clearly, my heart belonged to someone else. I found a million reasons to not sit and be with God. I had so many better things to do other than start my day with the creator of the universe. How did I not know that I had given my heart away . . . to the world? How could I miss that how George was rejecting my love was exactly what my actions looked like to God?'

Broken and fragmented, I let the tears fall from eyes in true remorse.

How much I am like my son!

I was reminded of the story of Hosea. Hosea was a prophet chosen by God and, to his surprise (and all of Israel's surprise), he was called to marry the prostitute, Gomer. They had three children, each one's name representing a judgment that God would have on Israel because they turned their back on God. One meant, essentially, "I have no more compassion on you."

God—in this story—said to Israel, basically, *'despite everything you've done, despite the fact that I should have no more compassion on you, I'm still going to restore you.'*

Gomer had returned to her prostituting ways, her heart not attuned to her husband, Hosea, nor to God. God told Hosea to show her love, anyway. He had been called to love her, even at her worst. Despite Gomer's heart not being faithful, Hosea remained faithful to her. He found her in the city and brought her home.

We all look at ourselves like Hosea. I did. I thought I had to be the "good Christian girl," but we can't be good. We aren't. We are Gomer . . . and God loves us anyway.

Hear my heart when I say this, that person who does not return love is often me, just like Gomer. What strikes me are two phrases God shares in this story (and you really should read it for yourself) including; "expecting nothing in return," and "he is kind to the ungrateful."

I offer nothing to God. He does not need anything from me and yet, He loves me and then is compassionate toward me, even when I do not recognize what He is doing.

George did not recognize what I was doing.

What I want from George is all God wants from me. Yet, I still cannot seem to give all of myself to God. I have an adulterous heart that looks to the world to bring me pleasure and comfort. I rush to see how many "Likes" my cute picture of my girls received. I turn on the news to fix my addiction to pop-culture. I even hide chocolate in the kitchen so I can somehow feel better after a hard day. Very rarely do I find myself turning to the Lord just to sit with Him.

Yet, He still pursues me.

As I sat on the floor, I never felt more intimate with the Lord than at that moment. In His loving mercy, nothing He was saying was condemning and shaming. Instead, He was gently showing me myself. He was showing me, through that mirror held up to my face, that I can be stubborn and unloving most days, too.

A friend of mine once told me, "Ships are built in the safety of a harbor, but they are meant to go out to sea."

I was built in a safe place. I have loving, Christian parents who took me to church – for about eight hours on a Sunday once you added up Sunday school, worship, bell choir, youth choir and youth groups. I had amazing teachers and godly leaders pour into my life on a regular basis. Therefore, my "ship" was strong and sturdy. Or, so I thought. It is easy to stay in the harbor. Now God was asking me truly to be like Christ, to love like Christ, to serve like Christ, to show mercy like Christ. He was asking me to be willing to lose it all, to sacrifice all I once held dear. He was asking me to love the unlovable. Most days, I am being tossed about on the ocean, yet I was built in a safe harbor, so I know the ship is sturdy.

I have heard God whisper to my soul many times over the years of this storm on the waves, "Don't waste this experience I am walking you through. I am up to something you cannot see. Just wait upon me."

Like most twenty-first-century women, I hate to wait. But I have realized that, if I fail to wait upon the Lord, I will miss out on what He is doing with my life . . . with George . . . with my entire family! If I fail to wait, I will never see the tapestry He has been weaving for a decade now. If I fail to wait, I will stop changing, which means I will fail to look more like Jesus.

When God allows us to walk through a difficult time, we must not waste the opportunity to be sanctified. I can only learn what it means to hold on to Jesus by walking through dark days. I can only learn to have patience when I live with someone who challenges that very thing. I can only learn how to love the unlovable by parenting a child who most days does not want to admit he loves or needs me. I can only truly forgive when I am given opportunities to be betrayed.

Forgiveness; I thought I understood the word, the idea, and the benefits. Apparently, I had been hanging on to some bitterness and anger, and God had been dealing with that in my life for years. In fact, He would not let go of my heart until I completely broke and confessed my hard-heartedness.

I had been so burned. I'd had hope before, and then had that hope dashed against the rocks quicker than I could blink an eye. I had begged God to do a work; to heal this broken child's heart and mind. God was telling me He was doing a work, but frankly, it was getting weary.

Over the ten years of parenting George, we had been hit, seen things broken, been lied to, and called the police dozens of times when he ran away. We even cried our hearts out when George had a mental breakdown in the ER of our local hospital and were told he would have to go live in a residential treatment facility until it was safe for his return. And sadly, we've seen him arrested for assaulting us. Life has not been easy. I have held on to bitterness. I just could not understand why God would allow me to feel the pain of loving a child who did not return that love.

It so easy to go through the motions of being a Christian in North America and not truly apply the "red letters" of scripture. Jesus said, "But love your enemies, and do good, and lend, expecting nothing in return, and your reward will be great, and you will be sons of the Most High, for he is kind to the ungrateful and the evil." (Luke 6:35 ESV)

Jesus did not take it easy on us when He taught on forgiveness. "Then Peter came up and said to him, 'Lord, how often will my brother sin against me, and I forgive him? As many as seven times?' Jesus said to him, 'I do not say to you seven times, but seventy-seven times.' Matthew 18:21-22 As a follower of Christ, I am called to forgive ALL the time.

I realized I had not been doing a very good job of genuinely forgiving. I overlooked. I brushed things under the carpet. I said I forgave. However, in reality, my heart was just growing more and more calloused. Even despite victories in bonding between George and me, and moments of great behavior, I still held on to bitterness. I have been hanging on to anger and bitterness this whole time; not even letting myself celebrate the small victories for fear of everything inevitably falling apart tomorrow.

Then God dealt with me. God started by just gently chipping away at the anger, the calloused heart.

After church one particular day, I was standing in the kitchen and Joe said, "You know she loves you," when George walked in. He asked, "Who loves you?" and Joe replied, "You do! You love your mom." Then George smiled and walked over to me, giving me the biggest embrace he has ever given me and said, "Yes, Mom. I do love you so much."

That same day, I needed to pick George up from work. I got there a few minutes early so I decided to go in to talk to his boss, offering that George could work tomorrow since it was a holiday and there would be no school. However, I could not find George anywhere in the grocery store! In fact, there was his boss doing the job that George should have been doing, bagging groceries. I was furious. I immediately thought, "Oh, he clocked out early and is off at Five Guys or Taco Bell." Or, "I bet he is just sitting in the break room watching the clock for the last fifteen minutes not working!" Steaming, I went back to my Suburban and positioned myself so I was sure to see him coming not out of the grocery store, but rather the nearby fast food joints. Right on time he came walking toward the car, from inside the grocery store....with a different shirt on. He was smiling ear to ear when he saw me and as soon as he got in the car reported, "You know that huge thunderstorm? Well, I decided to help two old ladies so they wouldn't get soaked. I told them to go ahead and get in their car and I would load their groceries into the trunk. So, I got soaked. My boss gave me a new shirt because I was so wet."

A bit humbled, I started the car and we drove home. On the way, George asked me if I would plug in his phone because he wanted me to listen to his new favorite song by For King and Country. As the tune began, I immediately recognized the melody and sang along, "And they'll know we are Christians by our love, by our love. Yes, they'll know we are Christians by our love." Love. Do people even know I'm a Christian by the way I love? If anyone could have read my thoughts – or probably even seen my face, they would have highly doubted if there was any love. Honestly, I wasn't loving my own son very well and here he was, sharing this as his favorite song.

Believe it or not, I still was not willing to let go of the bitterness root in my heart. Joe and I were at church one night (he had to play the guitar) and my phone suddenly rang. The caller ID showed me it was George calling. I immediately defaulted to, "Great, he did something. He caused a fight or he got kicked out of our neighbor's house." With anger, I answered, "What happened?" "Mom? I just wanted to ask you if I could go to the pool? I'll take Anna and Lincoln, too. We are going with our friends. I thought calling you and asking you would be the right thing to do."

I lose it in the lobby at church. Why have I been so hard-hearted that I cannot even begin to see that God is doing a work in George's heart? If I'm honest, I don't believe that God IS actually doing a work in George's heart! But, that is what I have been praying for . . . for almost ten long years. I think I had come to a place of accepting that life as George's mom was always going to be filled with hurt and anger. But today, he was a delight.

And as the last song was being sung, the words struck me:

And show me who you are
And fill me with your heart
And lead me in love to those around me

George is the one. I needed to sing about God filling me with His heart to lead me to LOVE George.

I was feeling soaked in love . . . God's love . . . just as George had been soaked in goodness. And, as with George, my Boss, my God, clothed me anew.

God chose George to be in this family. God chose me to be his Momma.

My heart broke. More like shattered and I confessed to God my hard heart, my unwillingness to truly forgive the years of pain. And I wept.

Breakthrough.

It felt as if chains physically fell off my wrists. I could hear them crash to the floor as I let go of those hard years. There is a miracle in how far George has come, and someday he will have an amazing testimony to share of God's faithfulness and love. This, however, is my story. The story of a woman who saw for the first time how my unwillingness to be with God broke his heart. The story of a God who continues to gently pursue. And the story of a woman who finally "got it" and realized how much joy and freedom comes from fully forgiving. God purposefully brought this child into my life, not for his sake, but for mine. I didn't "reduce" him; knowing him has redeemed me to God.

Proper Tools

For breakthrough to happen, we have to have the proper tools for the job. What's in your tool belt?

When I started out, I had two tools: a wrench to get my husband out of jams and a hammer to keep my kids in line. Trust me when I say I needed a lot more tools than that—I needed some delicate tools—some tools with finesse! I needed tools for those hard to reach places and for problems that were oddly shaped. (By the way, in a family of thirteen, all of the problems are oddly shaped!) Unfortunately, the proper tools don't just show up in two days like Amazon Prime. In order to have new ways to live, talk, think, and act, you must seek them out, learn and then practice them.

YOU MUST DO THINGS LIKE:
- Read books
- Attend a marriage or parenting conference
- Take a seminar in person or online
- Listen to podcasts and educational radio shows
- Watch YouTube videos (not the kind with cats)

Proper Tools in your life may mean going to psychological or pastoral counseling, or taking anger management classes. It may mean learning how to budget and invest. Sometimes it means hiring a life coach. What it always means is that, when you realize what you're doing isn't working, you find what does and you renew your mind. You must be proactive in getting new wisdom for life and relationships and, when you are, it always leads to breakthrough!

By the way, if this doesn't sound "spiritual" enough for you, I want to remind you that God put the Book of Proverbs in The Bible. It is a book of practical wisdom for living, mostly written by the wisest man who ever lived! It is full of contrasts between wisdom and foolishness, and pragmatic advice. God knows that we need wisdom and tools for success and Proverbs is proof! In fact, it is a great place to start on your quest for the Proper Tools.

https://www.biblestudytools.com/blogs/inside-bst/a-31-day-journey-through-the-book-of-proverbs.html (A 31-Day Proverbs Reading Plan – Try it!)

JENNIFER BUCHHOLZ is a believer, wife, and mommy who loves to share real life with her friends and family. She is real and open about both the good and the bad on social media, so this book was a perfect opportunity to share her breakthrough and impact more lives. She desires her story to ignite hope to its readers. Jennifer resides in New Berlin, Wisconsin with her husband and two young children where she's able to spend her days educating and supporting other families on their journey of health and wellness through natural options. To learn more please visit **www.JenBuchholz.com**.

Breakthrough

13

YOU ARE MY JOY

Jennifer Buchholz

'I could jump out the window . . . no, I'd probably only get hurt but not finish the job. Slit my wrists? That's such a big mess for my family to clean up. How about some pills, ugh! I don't know what they'd actually do. I don't want to try and fail because then everyone will know. They'll think I'm just looking for attention and I'll become a bother. A burden. Another thing on the long list of worries my parents already have to deal with. I'd be even more cast out at school. It needs to be something that works, is fast, doesn't make a mess. Even better if it can look like an accident or like it was just a sad mystery what happened. Man, I wish I had someone to tell me how to do it. But I don't have anyone. No one can know I feel this way. No one wants to know how I feel. They don't have time for me. I'm not worth their worry.'

These were the thoughts running through my head late at night in my bedroom . . . at ten years old. My family was busy just getting by and I surely didn't fit in at school. The chubby, hand-me-down clothed, glasses-wearing, shoe insert wearing, awkward, introverted nerd.

When and where I grew up, mental health was not something we dealt with. I heard adults around me say things like *'well if they really loved Jesus, they'd have joy,'* or, *'they're just looking for attention and drama.'*

I felt so alienated, alone, and desperate. I struggled with my self-image, value, spirituality, and identity. I felt like there was nowhere safe to turn. No one I felt comfortable talking to. No way out. Suicide seemed like my only option. Just disappear and start over.

But I had those lingering questions. *'Would it really be a start over, a new beginning? Where will I really go? Do I believe in the whole Bible and God thing? If it is true, where would I go; heaven or hell? What if it's not real, I could just disappear to nothing? Be reincarnated as someone or something better? What if I come back as something worse? Was killing myself going to send me somewhere with the same pain anyway?'*

So, I began to listen. I grew up in the church. Sundays. Wednesdays. You name it. If something was going on, we were the first ones there and the last ones leaving. I knew my parents believed all this, but I wasn't so sure. Every other religion in the world seemed to have the same certainty. Everyone says their religion is the right one, their god is in control. Were they all true? None of them? Or one and everyone else was wrong? What if I'M wrong?

I wanted to end the pain so much, but I had to plan things out, so I couldn't finish it off until I was certain what I would encounter in the after. I started taking notes at church, opening my Bible on my own – marking it up, searching for the evidence and certainty my plan needed to complete.

Even trying my hand at this praying thing. Growing up in a Christian home, my parents were great about bringing us up in prayer. "Now I lay me down to sleep, I pray the Lord my soul to keep. If I should die before I wake, I pray the Lord my soul to take."

I don't think I will ever forget those early prayers. They were helpful to instill a routine in me, but that wasn't doing it for me anymore. After years and years, they felt like empty words just echoing the silence of no response.

What if I just try talking? Like in my own voice. No, not talking, screaming, crying out silently in the darkness of my room each night. I mean, I still had a bed time, but these are the kind of thoughts that don't let you get any sleep.

So I'd get hours to think and wonder, *'Is someone there? Do you exist? Do you see me? Do you even care? You say You are love, but I don't feel it from you. I don't feel it from anyone. Does anyone love me? Do you?'*

I don't know the day, I don't know the time, but I can recall everything about the moment that it all changed. Another night staring at the pastel wallpaper as if it held a secret message I must decode. Hours of chatter bouncing through my head. Tears streaming down my cheeks. And then all of a sudden it was as if everything stopped. I no

It was like God had come and just placed His hand on the top of my head.

longer heard the hum of my bedroom fan or the wind through the trees out my window. It was as if no one else existed on Earth, and it was okay. I felt the calm come. I *wasn't* alone. I could feel Him. It was like God had come and just placed His hand on the top of my head. The gentle touch of a father's love and care. Every muscle in my face softened, it worked its way down my body releasing the tension all the way out through my toes. e

I knew God and H knew me. And *loved* me! It was like I truly was a new creation. The old was gone and the new me had come through His spirit upon me. (2 Corinthians 5:17) He was with me in the pain and the renewing. His Word promised me that He would see me through it all. That He had plans for me. For the first time, I actually *believed* it, all of it. Plans of hope. Plans for a future. (Jeremiah 29:11) A future? Well I guess I need to stay alive if I want to see that. He created me and saved me, and I've got to see what He has in store.

That night I devoted my life to Him. I was so grateful to be heard and cared for. I thought, *'since you say there's a future I choose to live. And if I'm living, I'm going to have some fun.'* I started writing down my bucket list, right then and there. When times get hard it's good to check something off the list, or add something new, and remember how great this life can be.

Finally I had meaning and a future. Praise God. But it didn't magically fix my life. School was still hard. Family life was still complicated. But I could look ahead to better days and be grateful for the good in each day.

One thing I added to that bucket list was to get married and become a mom. As I grew older, however, I wasn't so sure. Don't get me wrong, I always loved kids and even volunteered with them throughout school. But I also valued my own time and space so I began to think maybe I wouldn't actually accomplish that item on the list.

But then one day I met this guy at church in college. He invited me out to fly a kite at the local park. Sounded simple enough, but the wind was *not* cooperating. He showed such patience and dedication to get that kite up and make my day. By the time he finally had a smooth flight an hour later, I knew I was going to marry him. And I also knew I wanted to have his kids and stay home to raise them. A *huge* change and shock to many people around me. But God likes to do that. Take our plans for life and flip them upside down. More often than not, He knows what we need more than we do, and I was ready to follow this new exciting vision for my life.

About seven years later we had just welcomed our second baby into the world. Our first was a sweet little girl named Hailey who was the easiest and happiest baby. A true celebration of new life and worthy of her name which means "Praise the Lord." I thought I had this mothering thing down pat.....Then when she was just fourteen months old, we brought home her new brother Aaron.

The transition the first time went so well and I thought going from one child to two would be just as smooth. Boy was I wrong. It was so much more than I expected, and multiple factors played a role in my downward spiral over the coming weeks.

We later learned that Aaron had a lip and tongue tie affecting his ability to feed and disrupting his digestion as well as an issue with subluxations in his neck putting him in pain and causing lots of crying. But on my side there was also the rush of hormones, lack of sleep, and inability to connect with this colicky baby boy.

The thoughts came back like they were fifteen years earlier, but this time they were supercharged by the complexity of being a wife and mother. It wasn't just about me this time.

My eyes clenched shut, hiding from reality. But my eyelids alone couldn't shut out the chaos around me. My tiny newborn screaming at the top of his lungs. He was longing for comfort and love, things I couldn't give him today. Hailey's toddler toys blaring. "Welcome to our learning farm, there's so much to do." Oh how I *loathed* that tune, but it kept her out of my hair. It was too much. I blindly reached for the remote and turned the cartoons up louder to drown it out.

My hands clamped tight holding the afghan over my head. I could smell it. The beloved purple blanket my great aunt made for me when I was just a little kid. It still smelled like my parents' home. Those were the days, I thought. It reminded me of the first time I heard the horror story on the news. I was so young and innocent as I watched the reporter describe how a mother took the life of her two young kids. She had drowned them in the tub – a son and a daughter. *'How could she?'* Now I totally understood her. It seemed like such a logical thing to do. Like it was plain common sense. Something's broken. You fix it.

As the King of Lies screamed in my ear that my son, *"ruined your life!"* I imagined how the mother must have felt. She just held her children under the water until they finally stopped crying. She could enjoy the silence – just leave them lifeless and get back to the things she loved and that gave love back to her. Children are small and delicate. It probably didn't take much to get the job done. Satan even showed me images of smothering my own child. *"Everyone knows you're such a good mom to Hailey, they won't even imagine it was intentional."* Like crashing waves, he sent awful, murderous images. *"Everything was wonderful before he came along. Just go back to the way things used to be before the little terror arrived."*

Thankfully, the Spirit was still in me, at least giving me enough clarity to realize that those acts wouldn't end joyfully. I'd forever separated from the life I longed for. The tears pooled so much in the corner of my eyes that I

Thankfully, the Spirit was still in me.

couldn't keep them closed any longer. I open to blurry visions through the windowpanes of the afghan. The room was dark, as I kept the curtains drawn all day, but I could see just the top of Aaron's playmat that was lying next to the couch. His frustration made the whole thing shake as he strived for attention. I could smell his overly saturated diaper from two feet away, but getting up seemed impossible.

The short moments of sanity would soon be drowned out by the returning malicious lies from the evil one: *"Forget about the baby, you're the one who really needs to go. Your anger and frustration is affecting Hailey now, too. Look at her flinch when you reach for her. You're no good to any of them. They'll be better off without you. Your husband can just hire a nanny who will love them and raise them better than you could anyway."*

I think every little girl imagines being a mom. This life was so far off from what I imagined it would be that finding that joy again seemed useless. I let the hopelessness win and just rolled over, burying my face into the back of the couch.

Those were dark days. Mostly a broken record of crying, hiding, surviving, and internal battle. I'd place my daughter in her playpen surrounded by favorite toys to keep her contained and away from my sorry self for hours at a time.

My husband would arrive home to two needy children, both with dirty diapers. They were needing to be fed, loved on, and put to bed. He'd find me in any state from staring blindly ahead and unresponsive, to crying every tear in my body, to raging and slamming doors, to screaming at him under no fault of his own.

When my son was six weeks old, I had enough coherency to hear God reminding me that His mercies are new every morning (Lamentations 3:22-23) and I mustered up the strength to return to my moms' group at a local church. I silently listened to the speaker and small group discussion. I have no idea what it was about, I wasn't even trying to pay attention. I just remember sitting there. Trying to hold my son and look like I wanted him in my arms. Focused on maintaining my composure and not running out. Anxiously waiting for the lunch after.

You see, there was another mom in the group. I didn't know her very well, but she had been vulnerable enough to share her struggles with postpartum depression years earlier.

She had two daughters and she had gone from being a "GO! GO! GO!" woman to withdrawing into her shell, shutting out the world, and not being her "normal" outgoing self. It had affected her for years before she felt like herself again. BUT . . . *she did feel like herself again*!

I couldn't wait to get to her. God was pulling me to hear His hope through her. God never intended us to do this life alone, and He loves to surround us with our faith family when we are in need.

At lunch I handed Aaron off to her and my cousin 'so I could eat' (really just to get him away from me). I mustered up the words "so remember how you shared your struggles after your second was born?" She confirmed and asked what about it. Failing to fight back the tears I blurted out "how did you get better?"

I cry even now remembering her face and coming right to me – such empathy straight from one mother to another. She prayed over me, but I don't remember the words. I just remember her comforting me and letting me know it will be okay. She said to call my doctor and let them

Such empathy straight from one mother to another.

know how bad it's gotten. When I returned home, I was able to do that (through tears as well). They didn't even ask me to come in and sent a prescription to my local pharmacy. My husband was able to pick it up on the way home for me to start.

I remember the feeling after it kicked in. It was a feeling I have never before experienced. I was in a dream all day long, a fog. I went through the motions of a day like I was a robot. It helped with my aggression, but it lessened every emotion all together. I was indifferent to my kids – no laughing or fun – but at least I was able to feed and change them . . . cover their basic needs.

My prayers were very short back then. Short and blunt. I just said: "Help," or, "Remove this from me," or, "Let me make it through this day, or even just this hour."

A few months prior to all of this, my friend had created a new moms' Facebook group. It was focused around more natural living for health, home, and children. I was not interested in all this nontoxic, organic, crazy-expensive, hippy-dippy stuff. But she was my friend and I stayed to be supportive and I did enjoy the community it created.

If you have seen my house, you'd see I'm a Pinterest fan. And let's be honest, scrolling Pinterest for hours was an easy way to help make the day go by. All these do-it-yourself, household recipes kept making their way into my Pinterest feed. Candles, body butter, you name it. It was crazy how many of them had essential oils in the recipe. As I was trying to force myself to get back to life, I decided I would make one of these recipes.

'*Just pick an easy one and get it done. Do something, anything to get off the couch.*'

I looked online and was overwhelmed by the choices of these oils, but I couldn't avoid them any longer. '*The moms group will know,*' I thought. So I created a post asking what essential oils people liked best. A nice smell and reasonable price.

The response was overwhelmingly one-sided for these oils. One stranger commented "I'm having an essential oils class near your neighborhood tonight. You should come."

Yikes, a room full of strangers. A bunch of moms who probably have it all together. I can barely even stand my own family right now, how could I face them? I'd have to put on clothes, ugh, probably even some makeup, but I couldn't fight the feeling that I needed to go. God was basically pushing me there and I knew I just had to attend.

I went, intending to sniff and leave and talk to as few people as possible, but as she explained how they used each of these little bottles in their family I was thinking, '*Oh I need that one; this one smells amazing; that's interesting.*' Before I knew it, I had this whole box of aromas arriving to my home.

It came with one oil blend specifically formulated to support emotions. By this point I believed they were of good quality and a good price point and smelled great, but I did not believe they actually did anything for our bodies. I mean, I was raised by a nurse. We go to doctors and medicine for help – not plants. I mean, that sounds ridiculous!

"Well it can't hurt," I said, and gave it a try.

Now, if I was going to try something new, I was going all in. Like a scientific experiment, I wanted to be consistent. So I set an alarm on my phone. I created a routine of topical and aromatic use while incorporating praise song lyrics and prayer for change, that I would repeat every two hours.

The first two days, I was feeling relatively the same, but the third day there was this shift. A change in how I woke up, how I looked at myself in the mirror, how I responded to my children. Over the next week, I began to enjoy things again . . . . have fun with my kids, do things around the house, go for walks around the neighborhood, talk with people. I got my smile back!

I remember feeling so proud of myself as I got showered, dressed, made breakfast, and flung the curtains open. Heck, I even opened the windows knowing my neighbors would hear only joyful sounds. My yard looked so green and full of life. I had forgotten how the sunshine and fresh air just filled my soul. While I had been battling within myself, I hadn't even noticed that winter had turned to spring bursting with new life. God is such an artist in nature and it always helps me feel His beauty and attention to detail.

I looked down into my arms. There was this tiny baby with his dimple chin and big blue eyes staring deep into me. *'Aaah,'* it was like my mind took a sigh of relief. The softening fell on me. It took a while for me, but the tightness was gone. *'He is good,'* I thought. My son is good. And He is good. My God is good. I finally truly saw both for the first time. Aaron's little toes were moving in his pajamas and he was so cute. I loved him. My son. He was mine, a part of me. He must have felt so alone those first few months. I wonder what was going on in the minds of my littles as I came back to them. *'Did God send us a new mommy?'*

I could hear the tune of *You Are My Joy* by David Crowder Band.

Wait – was that humming coming from me? You *are* my joy. How appropriate as God had allowed me to once again be made new and filled with His joy. The kind of joy that isn't about being happy about something good, but that joy that is found deep within through His love and blessings.

Wow! Could this crazy stuff actually be helping? I was able to come off my medicine and, praise the Lord, not return to since. That alone wasn't enough to convince me. How could a little smell help me? I mean, that's just crazy . . . isn't it? Into the research, I dove. Who knew there were scientific studies done on all kinds of essential oils. Turns out this wasn't just a placebo effect. The chemistry is evident. If I believed in science, a gift of God, I had to acknowledge the power of the compounds found in these little wonders.

Again, I held myself back from being all in. I mean what was I getting myself into? I remembered back on the warnings of the wise as I moved away from home at seventeen years old. I was told to have caution of being overtaken by the ways and ideas of this world. New age. Voodoo. Whatever you want to call it, was I treading in a grey area that didn't align with my devotion to God?

Was I treading in a gray area that didn't align with my devotion to God?

How silly that sounds to me now. After all, what were the first gifts to the baby Jesus? Gold, frankincense, and myrrh. The more I looked, the more I found essential oils all throughout the scriptures.

From anointing to healing, they are intertwined from beginning to end. It was almost as if God wasn't just reassuring me that they were okay to use, but that it was where He wanted me to turn. He created nature in its entirety for us, including supporting our mind and bodies. These were God-given gifts to be used alongside prayer. (Ezekiel 47:12, James 5:14)

This was such a new idea to me.

Was this the *help* that I had prayed for?

To me, it was such a "God thing." He plopped me right with a group of strangers who had what I was looking for and, since then, they've become such a support system for me. They are all strong Christians, believers, and encouragers that I never would have met otherwise. Not only did God choose to answer my prayer of

195

removing something painful from me, he *replaced* it with something joyful.

It took time and prayer to continually open up to and experience this joyful life. It shifted my whole view of caring for my family. As the guardian of the home and our health, it's been quite a journey as we shift how we clean the home, what we eat, how we support our bodies, while honoring God.

I love remembering Romans 12:1 where the Apostle Paul writes *"Therefore, I urge you, brothers and sisters, in view of God's mercy, to offer your bodies as a living sacrifice, holy and pleasing to God— this is your true and proper worship."*

Our bodies are part of His holy creation and deserve to be treated with love and care. We need to remain thankful to God for our body, and choose to serve Him through how we treat it.

This enlightening path led to, not just a renewal of me as a mom, but also as a servant of the King. He used something I had never heard of to change my life and give me a new ministry. What a blessing it has been to hear people say that they see me as a completely different person than I was five years ago. For I know it wasn't my doing, but God healing me and showing me my true purpose here. It's a purpose in which I get to share hope and healing with His people.

My purpose has challenged me way outside of my introverted comfort zones, but, when you know what's possible, you can't keep quiet. He continues to call me to spread His healing with His beloved family. The modern church is aching for sound minds and bodies of health which are needed to continue the important work of furthering His kingdom to all the ends of the Earth.

I thought that when I found Jesus for the first time in my farmhouse bedroom, I had been made new. Indeed I had, in salvation, but I have since learned that it doesn't stop there. That's just the beginning. God wants us to keep seeking Him and growing. Our forgiveness and eternity is secured in that instant, but becoming more like Christ and doing His work here on Earth is everchanging.

Lesson by lesson, season by season, piece by piece He is continually making us new if we can listen to His hints of where to work next. (Romans 12:2) Either in our physical body, our thoughts and mind, our career, ministry, or family. Wherever God is challenging us to step out next is where we must go. Where are you ready to be made new?

"Therefore, if anyone is in Christ, he is a new creation. Behold, the old has passed away, the new has come!"

2 Corinthians 5:17

HEATHER TAYLOR's writing career started at just sixteen and today she is a two-time Amazon #1 Bestselling Author. Heather serves as the *Lead Ambassador for FEW* (the Fellowship of Extraordinary Women), due to her endless support, encouragement, and belief of FEW's mission to help women be extraordinary and tell their stories. Heather uses her in-your-face sense of humor to speak to women and teen girls who are trying to tackle obstacles like depression, self-esteem and relationship struggles. Her relatable personality and huge heart make it easy for her to offer compassion and hope . . . with a side of laughter. Heather's first love is her family. She loves playing with her granddaughter, laughing with her three adult children, and her thirty years of morning coffee dates with her husband, Terry. For booking information please contact: **hjtenterprise@gmail.com** and visit: **alliknowis.net**.

Breakthrough

14

WHAT DO YOU WANT TO CHANGE?

Heather Taylor

I was in the middle of my world breaking when I got my breakthrough. It wasn't a bright light or a giant arrow pointing to a big red sign. It came in the form of a friend I hadn't seen in a while, sitting on a hotel bed, wearing matching pajamas and asking me "What do you want to change in your life?"

I had been lost for almost two years by that point; I didn't really know how or what could help me, but I knew I had to do something. I wanted help so badly that I asked my husband to fly my friend, who was a life coach, to Tampa from Wisconsin for my birthday because some part of me, however small, knew she could help bring me back. She was, after all, the person God used to bring me back once before.

My husband also wanted me to get help, so badly that he begged her, secretly, to "please, help her."

My life had changed dramatically in the two years leading up to my break and I knew the reasons why. I was in constant pain, emotionally inside, and physically on the outside. My bones ached and my joints swelled with no real diagnosis for the symptoms. I had truly lost all hope of ever being better.

With as much pain as my body felt, my heart suffered even more.

We left our home of seventeen years in Pensacola, Florida to move to Tampa, Florida and, by doing so we left behind my daughter, Brooke, who—at the time—was emotionally broken, as well as a granddaughter. The granddaughter, up until the time we moved, lived with us for most of her life. I was emotionally devastated and physically broken.

There wasn't anything I could do. We no longer had the house in Pensacola; we already paid for the house in Tampa; everything was set up for the move. I had to go.

Until a month before the move, Brooke and her family were coming with us. Then her husband dropped the bomb.

He wasn't coming

He wanted a divorce.

He was fighting for full custody.

Brooke couldn't leave and neither could my granddaughter. All our plans, hopes, and dreams of starting a new life in Tampa, closer to my aging parents and to my other daughter, Lyn, who was moving there for college, were now gone and replaced with dread.

The situation changed overnight. I don't think it was a coincidence that the day we moved from Pensacola it, ended up experiencing the single highest rainfall ever in a twenty-four-hour period. Roads flooded, houses flooded, and our hearts flooded with non-relievable ache and torment.

We kissed our beautiful granddaughter goodbye for what proved to be one last time in a cold, empty garage that was beginning to flood from the rain. My husband and I both knew this would be the last time we would see her big, bright, blue eyes looking back at us. She was so confused and she looked at us for reassurance. We had to be brave. Her wild orange-red hair poking out of her big, yellow raincoat drew me in one last time. I squeezed her tight and inhaled for as long as I could until my lungs would no longer allow me to capture her scent, before they began to burn and tighten. I deliberately defied my body and waited an extra second or two to exhale, knowing I would never be able to remember her smell. The next time I saw her, if there was ever going to be a next time, she wouldn't be a baby anymore.

We left that rainy Wednesday with an emptiness in our hearts that I can only describe as the pain you would feel from losing a child. For all practical purposes, we did lose a child that day as her father ultimately won custody and has kept her from us, since.

We drove away from the home where we had spent the last seventeen years raising our family and making memories. The noise the U-Haul truck made was deafening, but it masked my uncontrollable sobbing and gave all of us a good excuse to be silent.

Arriving in Tampa was bittersweet. We had already picked out a beautiful two-story, 4500 square foot house large enough to accommodate my family of five and Brooke's family of four. Perfect at the time when we found it, the house was now entirely too big and a very painful reminder that they weren't coming home. Once again there was nothing I could do. It had already been paid for and contracts had already been signed. It was ours whether we liked it or not.

> *Perfect at the time we found it, the big house was now entirely too big and a very painful reminder that they weren't coming home.*

We did not.

During the first few months in Tampa, we all tried to adjust and start our lives over moving forward. It was a hard time, but things needed to be done. I was continually getting worse physically, so my husband insisted that I find a Rheumatologist and "find out what the hell is going on!"

When I finally did go to the doctor, I was very surprised to hear him say that he felt I had been misdiagnosed by my last Rheumatologist. He didn't feel like my symptoms were that of Rheumatoid Arthritis (RA), but Fibromyalgia. Without running any test or even looking at the past tests that had already been run, he was completely confident in his diagnosis.

In my heart, I really didn't agree with him, but RA is a very damaging autoimmune disease and the medicine you take for it is just as serious, so I welcomed the idea of not having it. We discussed options for pain relief and he recommended pain medicine along with a new drug that had just been approved by the Food and Drug Administration (FDA) for Fibromyalgia. I willingly accepted his course of action because anything, in my opinion, was better than RA and the medicine that came with it. When you're on an RA treatment plan, it's an ongoing process; weekly injections and daily steroids just to control the symptoms. I didn't think there was anything less pleasant than that.

For the next couple of weeks my family and I worked toward a common goal: trying to create a "happy" life in a new city, new home, and new school, while suppressing the agonizing pain and complete void that lay deep in our hearts.

My daughter, Lyn, and her fiancé were busy getting ready to start college and my son was preparing to start high school. My husband was hard at work like always and then there was me. I was quietly slipping away from my family into my own reality.

What I was experiencing was what anyone would expect to feel, emotionally, after everything that we'd been through. It was a natural, normal occurrence and we expected our feelings of sadness. But then, this new diagnosis and medication was about to change all that.

I didn't know it at the time, but I had slowly, but quite surely, been poisoning my brain with the new medicine the doctor had prescribed to help me.

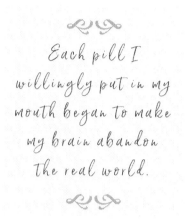

Each pill I willingly put in my mouth began to make my brain abandon the real world.

Each pill I willingly put in my mouth began to make my brain abandon the real world and create my own world of emptiness. Because I was coming off a natural sadness, we didn't recognize this drastic change as it approached. The depression started off slowly, with mood swings every now and then. Eventually it ended up becoming an armor of nothingness.

I lived in a cold, empty, emotionless void. It took every ounce of me to continue the facade of being me, and I really didn't do a very good job.

By the time I realized that something was missing, as in – my entire personality, it was too late. I didn't really understand why I felt the way I felt; I only knew it was too hard to keep trying to *appear* happy. I *wasn't* happy; I was miserable. I hated life, I hated fun, I hated feelings, I hated marriage, I hated my husband (because I felt sure he hated me), and most of all . . . I hated *myself!*

I was diving inward more every day, deliberately isolating myself as much as I could.

My daughter was planning her wedding and I was useless. I would sit in on the planning and try so hard to be happy for her, but she knew I wasn't really there. We weren't fooling one another.

My husband would try and rekindle our marital connection and I would start fights that always ended up with me telling him he should leave me.

I had created an iron wall around my fake reality. I can't really remember a lot of what happened during that two-year time period, but I know most of it was bad. I had enough real pain and loss to drag the strongest person down during this time, but—combined with a drug that literally gives you a false sense of reality—I didn't stand a chance. Well, that would be true, if there wasn't a God!

Reality hit. In July of 2015, my iron walls started to crumble. We planned my daughter's wedding shower and bachelorette party in Pensacola, Florida because the majority of our family and friends lived there. We rented a beach house for the week and invited the bridal party to come and stay with us. It was a crazy week-long party that everyone seemed to enjoy. Everyone but me. I tried to enjoy it. I tried to be the life of the party. I tried drinking my mental torment away. I tried a lot of things, but nothing worked. I found myself constantly looking around the room and wishing I was gone. I didn't fit in. I didn't want to be there. I was exhausted from trying to fit in and failing so much so that my husband and I barely spoke to each other anymore. My oldest daughter didn't even want to be in the same room as me. I once again found myself fantasizing about being gone.

Simply being gone was becoming a new obsession of mine.

I wanted to opt out of life.

Just as I was deciding how I could escape reality forever, my youngest daughter came up to me and said "Mom, I know you aren't happy right now, but I love you and none of this would matter if you weren't here. Thank you for making all of this happen and for loving me. I just want you to get better, Mom, so you can be happy again."

Simple, and yet, so powerful. She saw through my bubble. She knew I wasn't there. She saw me. I don't know why or even how, but those words penetrated through to my soul and gave me something to fight for. She deserved to have a Mom. I had to find out what was wrong with me and get it fixed. I wasn't going to leave. I was staying but I wasn't staying like this! That night I decided to do the unthinkable again . . . *pray*! I was in a beautiful home on the beach laying in an empty bed when I called out to Him.

"God, I know it's been a long time since we've talked. I'm not going to lie to You, as if it would do any good, I've been pretty mad at You lately. I hurt, so bad..." Tears began to paint a path down my face as I continued my monologue to The Almighty. *"I didn't think I could stand the pain of losing my granddaughter but I'm still here, so there must be a reason. My daughter needs me to get better, Lord. I need to get better for her. Please, I'm begging You here, please fix me or at least show me how to fix myself. I'm broken, I'm so broken, God. Help me."*

I cried myself to sleep that night not knowing that God lit a fuse in me that wasn't going to burn out.

When we got back home to Tampa, I decided to ask my husband for a birthday present. I asked him to fly a good friend of mine from Wisconsin to Tampa. I confessed to him everything that I knew was wrong with me and some suspicions I had about things I thought could be wrong. He looked at me with amazement and began to cry. He cried like the weight of the world had been on his shoulders. He was so relieved to hear me just admit there was a problem. You have to remember that I had basically spent the past two years trying to get rid of him, so this was a huge relief. We spent the rest of that night talking, crying, and making plans to fly my girlfriend to Tampa. I knew I had a very long road ahead of me but, for the first time, I felt like there might be hope, and that was all I needed to keep going.

I still had no idea, at this point, that the medicine I was on was a very big factor concerning what was going on with my brain. It would be almost a year before I completely understood this piece of the puzzle.

When my friend's plane landed, I was a bundle of nerves. I was scared of offending her by my new lack of, well, everything. I needed to be on my best "fake me" and not make her feel ignored or unwanted. Those were two things I apparently became really good at making people feel.

My husband had made hotel reservations for my friend and me so that we could have alone time. He gave us each an overnight bag filled with snacks, fruit, other fun stuff and even matching pajamas.

I was excited, nervous, cranky, and dying for a cigarette when I got in the car. My husband walked my friend around the car and helped her put her luggage in the trunk. I later found out he asked her to "please, fix her!"

Seeing me for the first time in over a year had to be surprising to her. I had gained a lot of weight, and I had already been quite big. I lost my front tooth, I was smoking like a chimney, I stopped wearing makeup, my hair was growing out and very unkept, my face was swollen, and I had an overall appearance of misery. She was kind and never mentioned my appearance. She never said a word when I left the room every ten minutes to smoke, and she didn't complain when, at 10:00 at night, I decided to go to sleep. I wasn't the fun girl who had the room laughing all night anymore. She knew who I was though, she knew where I had been and what I needed. She knew that God had called her to speak truth into my life and save me from myself, so that is exactly what she did.

"What do you want to change in your life?"

Her question was so sincere. She truly wanted to know what it was that I needed. I knew she wanted to know because that is who she was. She cared. I started to cry.

"I want to change everything. I don't want to be this person anymore, I don't want to keep suffering and making people around me suffer."

I could see her eyes start to fill up. She could see my pain and it hurt her. I remember thinking to myself we should have booked the room for longer!

"I have a chart I would like to fill out with you. It is just to help us see where you are and where you want to be. Are you willing to do it with me?"

"Yes, I am." Those three words began a process that would take over a year to complete.

Filling out the chart wasn't as easy as it sounded. I had to rate where I was now and where I wanted to be in a year in my:

spiritual life, relationship, finances, marriage, professional, health, and emotional health. The results weren't pretty.

Circle of Personal Perspective

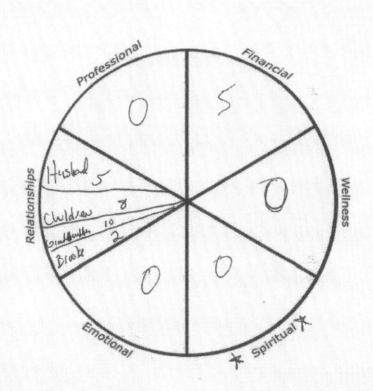

On a scale of 0-10, (0 being completely unsatisfactory and 10 being thoroughly satisfied), decide where you perceive yourself to be in each area of your life at the present time. Write that number in the appropriate area of the circle.

My scores were as sad as my overall state: Spiritual = 0/10; Relationship = 2/10; Marriage = 2/10; Health = 0/10; Emotional = 0/10

I was a mess. We spent the day mapping out changes I needed to make and plans on how to make them. There were so many things I needed to do to get back to who I was, but I had taken the first step. I

I was a mess.

had made my *first* breakthrough. I asked for help and got it. My plan focused on moving forward step-by-step and not looking back on past failures.

I started to renew my relationship with God and surrendered my life and my family over to Him.

I began a journey to healthier living. One of the things my coach shared was that I should look at the drug I was on for Fibromyalgia. I was a little upset. Nobody understood my pain. How could she think I didn't need it? I was actually a bit offended. (The devil will use anything to get in your head and the medicine made me delusional, so I assumed everybody was out to get me.) What she was saying made sense, though.

So, the very first thing I did when I got home to work on my health was to look into the medicine I was on and make sure that it wasn't causing any of these unwanted feelings I was having. I discovered fairly quickly after our sleepover that the medicine I was on was toxic to my mind and soul and decided to get off of it. There were major side effects from not tapering off gradually. I went through them willingly to get it out of my system as quickly as possible. What I did was foolish, and I would never recommend anyone do it that way. The pain can only be described as blazing hot pokers being tracked down my body over and over again. My mind was filled with delusions, I was overwhelmed with fear and anxiety, I was completely paranoid, bedridden, and unable to rest. Everything hurt all the time. I was in my own personal hell, but God gave me the strength to go through it. I never had any doubts that I would get through the withdrawals. God wasn't going to abandon me . . . *another* breakthrough in the midst of my breaking.

I was very blessed not to end up with long term side effects from not properly tapering off of that medicine. We found out months later that this particular drug was known for its horrendous side effects. If only someone had made me aware of that before I was put on them.

After the pain of withdrawal, the other things on the list fell much more easily into place: quitting smoking, losing weight, eating better, addressing major dental work that I had put off for years, finding, booking and following through with doctors' appointments, going to therapy for myself and with my husband. I repaired relationships that had been broken and evaluated relationships that weren't producing healthy fruit. I became healthily guarded about who and what I allowed in my life. I learned how to establish boundaries. I was feeling better and healthier than ever before, walking with God, attending a wonderful church, and pouring into my marriage, again.

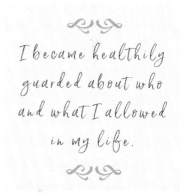

I became healthily guarded about who and what I allowed in my life.

My daughter got married. I cried tears of joy at her wedding but— more importantly—I *felt* joy at her wedding.

With God's love and mercy, I was healing and growing . . . being made new.

> *"Therefore, if anyone is in Christ, he is a new creation; the old has gone, the new has come!"*
>
> 꿰 *2 Corinthians 5:17*

WHAT DO YOU WANT TO CHANGE

God wasn't done with my breakthrough story, yet. I didn't realize it at the time, but all these other breakthroughs were just milestones to the real breakthrough that was about to happen.

I was invited to come help the dear friend who had helped me with a Women's Leadership Class she was facilitating. After everything she had done for me, I was happy to fly there to offer my help in any way possible and to just hang out with my friend. I knew the class itself wasn't for me, it was for women who wanted to be leaders, but I was happy to sit in on it and support her.

I had planned to sneak in the back and be as unnoticed as possible, but my friend threw me under the bus right in front of the class!

She was making everyone stand up and declare the "Cultural Mountain" that they had been called to, the place where God wanted them to work - Government, Business, Media, Arts & Entertainment, Education, Family, and Religion. The other women all seemed so confident.

As I prayed before my turn, I could hardly believe what God was telling me to do. There was no way I was going to get in front of all those women and say that! I would be humiliated. Devastated. They would laugh at me. I would die of embarrassment!

'Oh Lord, please don't make me say this!' I thought as I walked to the front of the room, but the words came out: "I can't believe I'm going to say this, but God is calling me to Arts & Entertainment!"

I waited for the laughter. It never came. I waited for the slight remarks, but they never came. In fact, they nodded their heads and agreed.

One of them even said, "I can totally see that!"

"What? You can?" I wanted to ask or maybe I did.

These women, who I was so terrified of, encouraged me.

They stood with me.

They believed in me.

I was overwhelmed with this new discovery that God had chosen for me. Deep down inside, I had always dreamed of being in the entertainment industry, but I never in a million years thought of it as a real choice. I was too fat, too old, too anything else that was negative to be in the public eye. Nonetheless, God most definitely told me to pick that mountain.

I learned a lot of wonderful things that weekend. I learned that God's call on my life was much bigger than I could ever have imagined. I learned that the trials and tribulations I had gone through helped me. I learned that God loves me and I need to love me too. I learned that I am His masterpiece and a one of a kind, special treasure that He is going to use to bring light into this world.

> *"Not only so, but we also glory in our suffering, because we know that suffering produces perseverance; perseverance, character, and character, hope."*

> ꒰᷄ *Romans 5:3-4*

Each new lesson was a breakthrough for me. I was so humbled by what he was teaching me.

As I was showering before my trip back home, I started to worship God. I thanked Him out loud for the work He did in me. I thanked Him for, not just saving me, but loving me enough to make me better. I begged Him to use me as He saw fit and to make me His vessel.

I opened my eyes after praying and wiped away my tears. I looked at the wall and read these words, a sort of decoration that I had missed before:

> *"Of all the people on earth, the Lord your God has chosen you to be his own special treasure."*

> ꒰᷄ *Deuteronomy 7:6*

I was overwhelmed with love, thankfulness, and complete awe of my Heavenly Father. I needed to lie completely down and surrender myself to Him. I laid myself out on the bathroom floor, hands above my head, face straight down and tears pouring out. I wanted to lift my hands to praise Him, but in this position, it was impossible, so I raised my legs instead.

It is probably better not to recreate this vision in your mind, but at the time it was one of the most amazing things I had ever felt. Suddenly, an image of what I must have looked like popped into my head and I began to laugh out loud . . . a lot! Shame overcame me and I started to repent. I felt terrible that I had ruined this beautiful time of praise by laughing. Then, right there on the floor, completely naked and still wet from the shower God finished my Breakthrough!

"Why would I give you laughter if I didn't want you to laugh? Why would I make something pleasurable happen to you if I didn't want you to have pleasure from it? Why would I call you to do something you didn't enjoy? My gifts to you are laughter and joy so that you can spread laughter and joy."

I knew God had just released me from a very large stronghold in my life. He showed me that I didn't have to suffer to follow His calling and in fact He designed me to enjoy it so I would fulfill it!

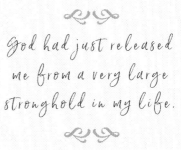

God had just released me from a very large stronghold in my life.

Since the day I made my chart, my list of the things I wanted to change in my life, I achieved all the goals on the list, weight-loss, managing health challenges, and building self-confidence. I even began doing a radio show – working on my cultural mountain! I used to be very guarded, but God calls people like us . . . like me . . . to go out and entertain the world on His behalf.

My breakthrough was complete! God brought me to the desert, led me to the land of milk and honey, and He was now showing me just how much He loved and adored me.

We are all made with a purpose and each one of us has a different calling.

I was broken; God took that break and turned it into a breakthrough!

JONI JONES has the overwhelming passion to share the hope, peace, and love of the Lord, that saved her from a lifelong battle of poor body image and the stronghold of bulimia. She is the author of Weightless Flying Free and founder of the ministry, *Be Waitless, LLC*, that encourages women to live out the Word of God in everyday life. Joni is a conference speaker, daily devotional blogger, and Certified Biblical Counselor. She loves being a wife, mother of three adult children, and a "Jojo" to her grandchildren at the New Jersey shore. Visit her website at: **www.bewaitless.com**.

Breakthrough

15

WEIGHTLESS

Joni Jones

I met her for the first time on the day I had to let her go: The Real Joni, who I kept well-fed and hidden inside. But something was tugging strong at my heart strings that gloomy morning in my kitchen as I sipped the last of my espresso.

Deep inside, I heard the words, "It is time. She is mine."

Paralyzed in fear, I thought *'Who would I be without her?'*, this little girl inside who was always there for me, whenever I needed a friend, comfort, and—most of all—love. And who could take care of her, as no one had in the past?

I got the answer that shook my whole body, "I will!"

My God, who carried me my whole life even though I didn't carry Him, will. My God, who brought me to this breakthrough moment to release this prisoner who had been caged in since the age of ten (the moment I began my quest for perfection) that lead me into a lifetime of bondage to food, diets, and—ultimately—a fourteen-year battle with of bulimia will. That's the God who would take care of her.

Once upon a time ago, this little girl was knitted together in her mother's womb and was fearfully and wonderfully made. If only she would have believed it. She was a sensitive girl, internalizing everything, taking to heart every wrong look or word, so "not enough" became her middle name. She subconsciously felt a constant

> Who God made her to be was in opposition to who others said she should be.

pressure and battle. Who God made her to be was in opposition to who others said she should be. Confusion set in. If what she felt or what she liked to do was criticized, then that meant that there must be something wrong with her. If she wasn't allowed to be who God created her to be, who was she then: rejected, insignificant, insecure? Therefore, she did the dance of perfectionism and performance to earn the status of love, but no matter what she did or didn't do, it was never enough. She decided to recreate herself, because the Joni that she was created to be would never, could never, be enough.

That little girl is now grown up with a playful spirit that I can't contain, as God restored all the years the locusts have eaten, plus so much more. He is so much more than our little hearts could ever imagine.

Have you ever felt invisible? Have you felt that you just don't measure up? This little girl exists in all of us. She exists in our lonely times, in our desperate times, in our hurtful times. What do you do with that little girl who just wants to be loved, held, and told that she is the prettiest girl on earth? If only you were more perfect on the outside, then you would be seen, heard, and understood.

I cry for that little girl who remained hidden for so long, hidden in clothing to cover her imperfect body; pretending to be sick so that she could stay home from school because her clothes didn't fit right; closing her eyes when she showered because it was she that she loathed. Her life broke down at the age of the ten the instant she overheard a comment that was she was getting chunky. It was at that moment when all her dreams of becoming perfect were shattered confirming her truth that she was not good enough. She concentrated on looking perfect to cover up the imperfection that was inside, hoping that, then—maybe, just maybe—she would be loved enough.

Breakthrough or breakdown moment...

The solution to her discontent popped into her little mind, '*If I can become the thin pretty one, then I will be loved.*' Her first innocent diet was birthed. When you think you find the key to peace, hope, joy and love, isn't that what becomes your focus? If only I was thin and pretty enough, then I would be loved enough.

There was a problem with this quest; her love for food was greater than any other love. Once it hit her taste buds, the overwhelming joy that radiated throughout her whole body numbed the deep-seeded darkness that she felt inside. Food became her best friend. Whenever the excitement she shared about her accomplishments were swept under the carpet, food was her companion. Whenever her legs were defined as big, or when no one would listen to her, it quieted her soul. Dieting became part of her lifestyle and so did excessive exercising and starving herself when she overate, because her mission was to look good enough.

Food, glorious food, was my innocent drug of choice to numb the deep-seeded emotions whenever they tried to emerge. I was afraid to feel – I believed that I would explode if I did. Could anyone tell that there was a constant battle inside of me? Oh no, because on the outside I appeared to have it all together, but if you looked inside you would know. Always seeking, yet never arriving, because I was seeking the impossible.

Food was my stronghold. The bible describes a stronghold as a safe place, a place of refuge that protects. Food was where I ran to hide. But no matter where I ran, I was still there. We all have those places we escape to when we don't want to feel where we are. They come in all shapes and sizes, from shopping, Facebook, anxiety, alcohol, to drugs. You name it. I was fighting a losing battle, yet I was persistent to reach my goal.

Breakthrough or breakdown moment...

Fast forward to college, when I over indulged in alcohol and felt terribly sick. A friend suggested to me that I purge. There was no way I could do that, but desperate times call for desperate measures. And I did. At that moment, a lightbulb went off. *'Yes!'*

I found the key to life. I would never have to diet again. It was fun. I could take this wherever I went. No one could take that away. I became Joni the bulimic. Back then, eating disorders weren't talked about. I didn't even know that what I was doing *was* a disorder. I found my new friend and no one was going to take her away. My secret. My love. My life. My god.

My first 'innocent diet' now turned into a monster. I truly believed that it was all about the weight, but today I realize that it was just a bandage I wore over my stuffed emotions. My new friend followed me for fourteen years, through marrying my husband thirty-five years ago, through the birth of three children, through moving nine times. It followed me, because wherever you go, there you are, no matter how fast you run.

Little did I know that God was weaving together my breakthrough story, beyond my wildest dreams. God never gives up on us.

Breakthrough or breakdown moment...

The bulimia started to take a toll on me after the birth of my second child, my son. Up to that point, for six years, I kept it hidden from my husband, until I experienced a mental and physical breakdown, as I was dehydrated, depleted of all nutrients. My husband, a gift from God, loved me through thick and thin and had me see a nutritionist. I thought it was all about the food, but I discovered that the food was just a mask I wore over my emotions. I then went to therapy, which uncovered many of the layers that were fueling the behavior, yet never enough to get to my wounded heart that still continued to find comfort with the food stronghold. I would only get so far.

On those nights when my husband traveled, and I was alone at night with the three kids, panic would strike me that I was going to die, as palpations filled my chest. I believed I was going to have a heart attack because of what I was doing to my body. *'Who would take care of my kids and my husband if I were gone?'*

How selfish of me, I would "swear" not to do it again. I was so thankful when morning came, as I had a new lease on life, but as soon as I was triggered, I was back to doing what I swore I would never do again.

There was something missing as I, in my own power, was working too hard and not getting anywhere. I was just controlling a behavior that was destroying me instead of providing me with what I thought it was intended to bring. It was bigger than I was and out of my control. I realized that I needed more than a nutritionist and a therapist to do the impossible, and set me free from this monster. I had enough of being not enough. I needed God who I thought I knew, when actually I didn't.

I would dream about the day that I would be free of the food stronghold. That day of freedom meant that Jesus would take it away *and* give me a perfect body. I actually wanted freedom for all the wrong reasons. I was more focused on simply getting rid of the behavior without changing my nature. I wanted God to reach His hand down and just stop me in the middle of it. So I continued practicing the behavior, as I waited for God.

God doesn't work like that. I was bowing down to my stronghold and not to my God. There is no room for idols in God's kingdom. He wasn't going to just whisk away something that I was busy honoring. I wanted the behavior changed and I didn't want to have to do anything.

'Why should I? I was the one suffering, wasn't I? I didn't put this on myself; it was because of others. Didn't I deserve to be free of this? God, prove yourself to me and take this away!'

Just as (I thought) I found a way to have my cake and eat it too, (a fitting analogy for my stronghold), I found my own theology. I kept worshipping my idol while waiting for God to heal me. What a bunch of lies that were in my head! Who was God? The God I was depending on was not the God of the Bible. I was a rebellious child full of pride.

I carried around the God of my youth. I talked to Him, but He wasn't in my heart. I strongly believed He existed, and Jesus was His Son, but I didn't know them. As I look back over my life, I see how God was constantly trying to get my attention, yet I pushed Him aside. He always placed a Christian in my life, wherever we moved, but I never thought twice about it because I *believed* I was a Christian too. My aunt and her family became Christians, and I used to laugh when I heard that they were praying for me, even before the bulimia. Well, those prayers were needed now.

Breakdown.

In desperation, I called my aunt and asked her what I had to do to find God. She lovingly found me a Christian church in my area. Little did I know that their prayers were finally about to be answered. Fearfully, one Sunday, I sought out the church. The music began. People clapped, people cried, people smiled. This was different than the church I'd grown up in . . . motions in church, happiness in church, why all the tears? It just happened to be a baptismal Sunday, so testimonies were being read, something that I never heard before. They shared their struggles, addictions, and, most of all, the transforming power of God. Wow, God can change people. I left there confused, yet hopeful.

Breakthrough.

I returned the following week and my heart opened up. I couldn't stop crying real tears over the hurts and the emptiness of the past. I could feel the pain that I had been hiding for so many years. I also felt the joy around me. Something was different about "their" God. The sermon blew me away. I never knew that what the pastor was speaking about was in the Bible. Actually, I didn't even know what was in the Bible. I didn't know that I needed the forgiveness that only Jesus offers. I walked out in a trance. Something was happening to me. I felt peace for the first time in my life.

I found God.

The door of my heart was opened when I gave it to my Lord. True healing began the moment I fell in love with the Author of Life, as I started to get to know Him. How vulnerable I became as I poured out my unedited heart to Him, sharing my deepest darkest secrets, feelings, hurts, and doubts. I did it through journaling letters to Him.

As soon as I wrote, "Dear Lord," I felt safe. I wasn't alone. God's presence surrounded me. I could share my heart with Him, my Creator. As I was honest with God, I was able to be honest with myself and others. God never left me. I was not alone. This was a God I could trust with me, myself, and I, not to mention the little girl inside.

I met a God who forgives, heals, redeems, and satisfies. I was finally able to rest in God's arms because He was my God, the God who made me, guides me, the God who works miracles in me. The God who is aware of everything about me. The God who loves me and who meets all my needs.

I met a God who forgives, heals, redeems, and satisfies.

And then I met His Son who wanted me more than anyone else ever wanted me, so much so that He died for me. I found my new partner in crime, who I could walk through life together with as He healed my wounded heart and loved me back together, piece by His peace. As I grew in my faith, I was able to shed the shackles from the past. I had a lot of baggage, but it wasn't too much for God. He began to heal those wounds of the past that I carried with me into adulthood.

God got to the heart that was eating me, the original wound from which rejected, insignificant, insecure Joni was born, at the age of fourteen, when she almost died of dehydration. Whenever this event was referenced, I deducted that it was my fault that it happened, and that I had caused my parents pain. This incident fueled the lie that I had to be punished for being who I was or who I wasn't. I became damaged freight, therefore I deserved to be treated as such. I was always told that I should be happy that I was alive because of what happened, which I internalized to mean that I caused it. But where were the *'I am so happy you are alive'* words that I so craved. God was saying it all along. Unless the original wound or hurt is healed, the present and future will be infected by its pain.

Breakthrough.

It wasn't my fault!

He never gave up on me, even when I wanted to. God is faithful. He never stopped loving me, even when I didn't love myself. I finally found the key that I was looking for. God began to put me back together. It was painful at times, but always worth it. Giving up the bulimia and the control I had over food was like giving up an old friend. I remember the day I was crying out to the Lord, when I could see and feel a little crying Joni, all curled up in a ball, inside my stomach. I felt that if I were to give up the food stronghold, I would be giving up myself. *'Who would I be without her?'* She was the only Joni I knew.

He never gave up on me, even when I wanted to.

God called me a new creation in Christ when I committed my life to Him, and that was where my identity could be found. Embracing the truths that God loved me and was with me always, removed the fear. It was at that point that I gave up the food stronghold and the little crying Joni to God, asking Him to fill the void that was left. He was right there. He became my comfort, my stronghold. It was at that point that I totally surrendered myself to the Lord, which began the process of becoming the Joni that He made me to be.

Breakthrough.

<u>Goodbye Old Friend</u>

When I was sad, I would run to you.
When I was lonely, you were there to bring comfort.
When I was frustrated, I could take it all out on you.
When I was angry, I could punish myself with you.
You were the lord of my life.
You were always there and I could use you
For whatever role I wanted you to play.
First bringing comfort, then pain.
You began to destroy me, yet I couldn't let you go.
I didn't want you anymore, but who else did I have.
Where would I go if I needed comfort, to hide, to protect myself?
Who could do what I allowed you to do?
I thought you could save me. I gave you way too much power.
It is time to say goodbye.
I found your replacement.
I found a place where I can go when my needs aren't met by others.
I found a place where I can go and be myself, and not be judged.
I found a place where I can run and be safe.
I found a place where I am always accepted.
I found a place where I can feel all of my emotions.
I found a place where I no longer fear.
I found a place where I am truly saved.
I found a place in My Savior's Arms.
So goodbye, my old friend, you are no longer needed in my life.
You have to go,
Because there is no room for other idols in my Father's arms.
He is all I need.
He is my fortress, my refuge, my stronghold.
He is my Lord.
Breakthrough Moment.
Hello, Little Girl.
Hello, Joni.

What a breakthrough moment when I had enough of being not enough. I had been set free.

I don't have to perform anymore to be seen, to be heard, to be accepted, because He saw me, He heard me, He accepted me the moment He came to me and lifted me out of the pit of shame, from the pit of not good enough, the moment He saved me from myself. I can still feel myself being lifted out of the quicksand that was sucking me down, further away from who I was born to be, deeper into who I thought I should be, a better version of Joni, a more lovable version of Joni.

That was just the beginning. Jesus broke into my life so that He could give me more than just one breakthrough moment, as He continues to write my story, as He isn't finished with me yet.

> *Jesus broke into my life so that He could give me more.*

Today, the little girl is now all grown up. I may have been set free from the monster of bulimia twenty-five years ago, but I always had it as a Plan B, just in case God was not big enough. Therefore, I dabbled with it through the years, when I felt hopeless and helpless. I would run back to my old friend, because it was still an option. My biggest fear has always been that, if anything horrible would happen, then I would go back to the food and the bulimic behavior.

Then, I found myself in the midst of a trying time in my family. It was overwhelmingly difficult and I assumed the old behavior would return, or at least a longing for it. Where was the food stronghold in the midst of the pain? Nowhere to be found. Even though I hadn't been practicing the behavior, there was always a small voice in my head reminding me that it was still there. But where was that thought? Nowhere! Actually, my stomach churned now just thinking about ever practicing the behavior again. It was forever gone! I experienced a freedom, in the midst of struggle, that I had never felt before.

God brought me full circle, from the little girl inside of me that he loved back together, just as He promised He would, to a woman free from any stronghold in her life other than the God who healed her. God always delivers on His promises. I found the One who sees, hears, and understands me. He makes me accepted, significant, and secure in Him. I am forever free from my breakdown to enjoy my breakthrough.

The little girl is now grown up, free to be the she that she was created to be because God added to her *Once Upon a Time* beginning. He brought the perfect ending to her imperfect story the day she met Him face to face.

> *Once upon a time there lived a little girl who was knitted in her mother's womb. She believed she was fearfully and wonderfully made, because three nails hung her rags of rejection, insignificance, and insecurity on the cross the day her real God wrote her happily ever after ending.*
>
> *Little did she know that, as long she pursued God, with her eyes fixed on her future hope, He would continue to take her from rags to riches with His three words, "I love you,"; words that hung Him on a cross.*

He did that for all the little girls. He did that for you. Come out of hiding.

Breakdowns lead to breakthroughs when you reach for a real God who is right there with you, to feel the depth of your pain, as He asks you to trust Him that He will be enough in every one of our not enough moments. My eyes fixed on Him is what enables me to press forward in this journey through life. He continues to write my story, as He takes me from breakdown to breakthrough on my way to the perfect ending that every little girl desires;

"And she lived Happily Ever After."

He promises.

Solid Support

To get your breakthrough, you need solid people in your inner circle.

WHAT IS AN INNER CIRCLE?

Let's call it your **Fab Five**—the five friends or confidants you spend the most time with. They are your inner circle because they have the most access to your heart, mind, and life, and you have access to theirs. Since human beings were wired to "rub off" on each other, this means that no one is rubbing off on you more than these five people. That is why your inner circle is of the utmost importance! Leadership expert, Jim Rohn, says that you will become the combined average of the five people you spend the most time with. This is true in attitude, health, and finances and it will happen in just three short years.

Who are the five people you're about to morph into? What are they like? Do you respect and admire them? Would you take their advice? Do they lift you up or bring you down? Think hard – because you've given them an exceptional amount of influence over your future. That is why it is imperative that we get around wiser, more successful, healthier people and let them rub off on us!

> *"If you want to fly with eagles, you have to stop scratching with the turkeys."*
>
> ～ *Zig Ziglar*

This final factor in the Breakthrough Formula is actually exponentially multiplied to more accurately reflect the powerful culminating affect human interaction has on other humans. When you choose to surround yourself with people who believe in you, speak life into you, and expect more from you, guess what! You will GROW! Unfortunately, though, the opposite is also true.

Choose wisely and choose well! Remember that four quarters is better than one hundred pennies. Don't be afraid to do an inter-personal detox and purge your life of toxic relationships at the same time that you pray new, solid support in. As you utilize all of the other breakthrough formula factors on a regular basis and begin to grow as a person, you will also find that you attract more solid people. You will be amazed at the person you become!

LISA MURPHY has a Bachelor of Arts degree in Criminal Justice and Spanish from the University of Wisconsin Eau Claire. She is also a Chartered Property Casualty Underwriter and has worked in the insurance industry her entire professional career. She resides in Hartford, Wisconsin with her two teenage boys, Alex and Quinn. Lisa works toward growing herself daily in her faith and desires to give hope to others that find themselves in the middle of a life storm. This is Lisa's first publication and she is grateful to be a part of such an inspiring and faith-based book. Lisa enjoys fitness, traveling, spending time with friends and family and attending *Northbrook Church*. Lisa can be reached at **lisamariemurphy19@yahoo.com**.

Breakthrough

16

THE DAY GOD REDIRECTED ME

Lisa Murphy

"Not only so, but we also glory in our sufferings, because we know that suffering produces perseverance, that produces character that produces hope.."

Romans 5:3-4

s I was lying on the hard, cold floor it felt like the life was painfully draining out of me and I was slowly going numb. I could smell the freshly installed hardwood floor and my limp body reflected off of it. The tears kept falling and my stomach ached like never before. It was the coldest January day in the history of my life. I was scared and paralyzed with fear.

'*Is this what a broken heart feels like?*'

I would rather have been shot at point blank range. Friends and family stopped by, one by one, over and over again to comfort and support me, but I kept falling back down to that familiar floor. The floor felt safe. You can't fall any further when you are on the floor.

Have you ever been told something by someone you loved and trusted with every part of your being that felt like a punch to your stomach? Within just seconds and a few words, a five-year relationship and engagement were ended.

I won't ever forget the words, "I don't love you and I don't think I ever loved you."

I literally curled up in a ball in the corner of the room. He said I was acting like a scared little girl. I certainly was. He seemed to be in shock as to how I was reacting. After doing some digging, I learned he was in love with someone else. The text messages I found and subsequent encounters and communications with them were brutal. We had only been in our newly built home for six months and his goal was to get me out, as soon as possible, so he could start his new life with his new family. My self-esteem was at the lowest I've ever known it to be. I felt like my two young sons and I were trash being put out to the curb. It was as if we never existed or mattered.

I kept repeating to myself, over and over again, as if trying to convince myself, *'I do matter. We matter.'* I now refer to that day as the day God redirected me.

From that hardwood floor, I spiraled into more darkness wondering how I would get out of this black hole that was really a frightening place to be. I knew the strong, independent, educated woman I built myself up to be, but I couldn't find her. Where did she go? She was obviously very lost. I had allowed myself to get lost in someone else, as if I had lost my own identity.

It was very dark and I was very scared.

Fear was completely taking over every part of me.

Being rejected was not something I could come to terms with.

Where does a forty-seven-year-old woman with two boys go? He just wanted me to go away, anywhere, just not be there and do it quietly. Our blended family was no longer. The boys and I were on our own. We had lost the future that I thought was solid. My fear continued to grow and my self- confidence was at an all time low. The darkness went on for months.

Our blended family continued to live in the same house; he and I slept in the same bed, night after night. We even went on a family vacation together with a group of friends. I was humiliating myself, but continued to be desperate for my life not to change. He just wanted me to leave

I continued to be desperate for my life not to change.

without confrontation, but I wasn't leaving. I found and emptied out a large bin full of cards, letters, and gifts he had given me over the five-year relationship and set everything out on a display to remind him of what I used to mean to him. I even posted notes on the wall outlining how I was going to change for the better. I was fighting for my survival. It was desperate . . . and pathetic.

I continued to be paralyzed by fear. I could feel my wings; they were there, but they wouldn't move. God was whispering to me that I was strong and could get through this, but I kept ignoring Him, instead wallowing in self-pity and grief, while getting used to the darkness which was becoming my new normal.

As the next few months went on, I sunk deeper into the pit, still desperate for my world not to change. I'd look up from that deep pit, but had no idea how to climb out. The climb out looked so daunting and the top too high to reach. How was I going to do it? The thought exhausted and overwhelmed me. Too much work, forget it, I'd tell myself.

I chose to stay in the pit.

So often during this dark time I'd fall to my knees and beg God not to change my life. I'd literally yell out, "Please don't let this relationship end! I'll change. I promise. I'll be better. Please hear me."

Deep down I knew what was happening was for my own good, but I didn't want to go through the pain of the break. It's a different pain. You can't describe it. You have to experience it to know it. So many people kept telling me, "You have to get over this, move on, and forgive." Well they weren't me and they weren't experiencing what I was. I know they meant well. I just wanted to get right to the end part of this experience, even though I wasn't sure what that looked like. The future looked foggy and frightening. I remember driving my car and thinking, *'If I would just veer off the road maybe the pain would go away.'* I wanted to trust God, but I didn't know how.

I had known God throughout my life, but not very well. My experience with God was an upbringing of attending church where routines and rituals were stringently followed, and I was told I had to participate. I never remember feeling inspired. It felt like punishment more than anything good. I was introduced to the Bible but not the content or meaning. I went through about ten years of religious education and came out knowing very little. Religion classes were usually held in dark, dingy basements and all I could think about was the class ending so I could get out of that depressing environment. I dreaded church and religion classes. I now realize how much I was missing because I wasn't listening or relating to any of it. I stopped going to church when I was eighteen. My relationship with God was weak and nearly nonexistent.

I continued to break. I stayed in bed for what seemed like years but was actually about a month. I'd sleep all day and lay awake all night, in familiar darkness, my mind racing endlessly. I took a leave of absence from work.

What? The workaholic wasn't working? I have a huge work ethic but working too much helped put me in this situation. Work came first, and the ones I loved and who meant the most to me came second.

I stopped eating, and a thirty-five-pound weight loss later, I reached my dream size of zero. I looked into the mirror and saw a skinny body, but a very empty person. The reflection I saw was a ghost. The brown eyes looking back at me were lifeless. I walked around like I was invisible. I was numb inside. Had I lost my spirit? I remember going to buy new clothes because nothing fit me anymore. I went into a clothing store, feeling very weak and defeated and telling the sales lady I needed some new clothes. She smiled brightly and asked me what the occasion was with a very excited voice. I was devastated. I went into the dressing room, sat on the floor (because that was familiar and comforting to me) and cried.

God continued to whisper to me, reminding me of my inner strength and telling me to trust in Him, but I continued to ignore Him, and instead listened to the devil tell me I deserved what was happening to me. The darkness and constant pain would not go away. I'd lose days crying and feeling sorry for myself. I was wasting a good life away.

I did not want my life to change. I was fighting God's plan for me every step of the way as my dark journey continued. Was I going to lose my new home that I had only lived in for six months? I did. Would I struggle financially? I did. Would I lose friends? I did. Would my two adolescent boys be heartbroken too? They were. I was scared to be alone and I felt completely abandoned by the person I trusted the most.

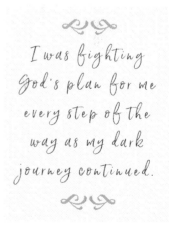

I was fighting God's plan for me every step of the way as my dark journey continued.

I looked for anything that would make me feel better and stop the hurt, any kind of band aid that would stop the bleeding. I was desperate for any kind of relief. I tried antidepressants, alcohol, one-night stands, toxic relationships, and more.

All of these indiscretions and very poor decisions helped me stay numb, but I knew that engaging in all these things was going to keep me in that dark hole that I so desperately wanted out of, and the devil wanted me to remain in. It's amazing how present the devil is when you are in your loneliest state. He kept knocking at my door and I continued letting him in.

> It's amazing how present the devil is when you are in your loneliest state.

I finally moved out of that five thousand square foot house that I had then lived in for a year. Although I had put a great deal of thought and effort into planning and building what I thought was my dream home and would be my forever home, I realized and accepted it was just a material thing. Two weeks after I moved out, he got married.

It wasn't rational to him. It was like he was living in a different reality from the rest of us.

I felt like I had been kicked in the stomach for a second time. I was so confused. He had only ended our relationship less than six months ago. He was moving on and I was living in the past. But it was not for me to understand. It was out of my control and I had to move on no matter how difficult that was going to be.

There is one thing I have always known about myself and that is that I'm a fighter. I was someone who never gives up. I needed a nudge... a big nudge! By God's grace He nudged me by surrounding me with women of integrity, faith, and strength. They picked me up, all in different ways. They included me when I felt so excluded and alone. We ran races, even a marathon. Running brought a sense of freedom and peace to me that became addicting. When I run, I imagine I'm running toward God, toward Heaven. And for a while the pain of running masked the pain in my heart, and then turned into healing for me, one step at a time, one mile at a time. We had coffee, went to concerts, and had regular outings. We also went to church. One of my friends would tell me what time she and her family would be there, and they would be waiting for me in the lobby. I'm so glad I did not let her down. I now enjoy going to church and don't like to miss. Sundays are special days for me because they start off with church. The list goes on. I call these women who were at my side providing me with endless support my angels on earth. The sounds of laughter, warm embraces, and conversations, when you are vulnerable are real and meaningful. We all have struggles, and when friends support one another in times of need, they help us to remember our wings so that we can fly. I am forever grateful for these friendships.

Then there is my sister, who has always been my rock. Through my break, she became my boulder. Each morning after the breakup she greeted me with kind words or a motivational text which often times included scripture. She did not miss a morning. I've always known God put her in my life for both good and bad times. She never gave up on me, not for a second. Our relationship has grown stronger and we have gone down the faith path learning together,. I will be forever appreciative of her love and support.

In the midst of the slow healing process, I crawled out of that dark hole. I found myself lifted up one inch, one breath at a time.

I will never forget hearing my fifteen-year-old son at the time say to me in a very gentle and caring voice, "Mom, it's time for us to go."

I found myself lifted up one inch, one breath at a time

How could such a young man have so much wisdom and kindness? He was a voice of reason breaking through the voices inside that kept telling me I couldn't move on. I would slip back from time to time but I continued to be nudged by God's grace and mercy.

I finally started to own my own truth. I found being the victim and blaming others for the break-up much easier than taking a look in the mirror and being honest with myself. I have since owned my own faults, one fault at a time. I had not been a happy person for a very long time. I was selfish, envious, impatient, judgmental, strived endlessly for perfection, and was mostly an ungrateful person. A girl that had so many wonderful gifts right in front of her couldn't see them, was completely blind to them. That's a tough person to be in a relationship with. I was a very poor distributor of grace and kindness.

I looked back to growing up with my two sisters in a strict home where there wasn't much room for being weak. My dad insisted we follow the rules and succeed. My dad was a Marine and worked in corrections most of his career. His rules were rigid. I do believe his intentions were good and he was doing the best he knew how to do, but the reality was that crying and weakness were for sissies, and if you struggled with something you toughened up and you figured it out on your own. I have now realized that weakness was what was right about me. It was actually acceptable to be weak when I thought it was not, because when you are weak you learn to depend upon God. That is the very power of weakness. In the dark you have immediate access to God. Turn to him to help turn your weakness into strength.

God brought me to a break in life and then guided and watched over me during the healing process so I would not miss out on a blessed life. I was stuck in a whirlwind of ungratefulness, and those close to me suffered immensely because of it. I have asked God to forgive me because it hurts my heart immensely that I allowed those I loved the most to experience this dark side of me. I hope they can all forgive

God brought me to a break in life and then guided and watched over me during the healing process.

me someday, including the man that ended our relationship that very cold January day.

I have also learned to forgive others and be empathetic to their situations in life. We are all sinners, but God forgives us so I believe we have the same obligation to forgive others. We all have a cross to bear. I believe people do the best they can with what they have in life. I am conscious of choosing empathy and kindness in my relationships with others.

One of my favorite things now is getting to know new people and listen to their stories, *really* listen to them.

I was so guilty of not being a good listener while I was in my own pain. I was missing out on knowing people, their stories, and what was going on in their lives. I now appreciate the perspective I have in life and share it with others. I have been in that dark place and have so much more appreciation for relationships now.

I don't complain about little things. The life I thought I was going to have was lost, so when I see people with stability in their relationships, I'm able to bring them that perspective without them having to go into that dark place on their own. My heart is more open to meeting people and listening. I've heard many things that I would never have heard before. I've learned to pray for what I want and to be kind to others. The prayer is for God to bring peace to my heart.

I have met so many wonderful people in just the last few years. I have formed new friendships that I put great value upon and do not take for granted, not for a second. My faith journey with God has been a gift I do not deserve but have been graciously granted and am so fortunate it continues to grow. I now focus on living in the present and waking up each day with a grateful heart. I look for signs from God constantly, both big and small, from a beautiful sunrise to my son asking me if he can join me at church.

My sons and I moved to a quaint little community with great neighbors that have embraced us and made us feel at home. We get together often, and I have new friends that have joined the ranks of women I already hold dear in my life. I had built a dream home once before, but now God has put me in a dream neighborhood where we are comfortable and feel like we belong. I am so blessed with true relationships, and to now be able to see and realize them.

One of my biggest gifts is my relationship with my sons that I may have missed out on had I not been redirected. I now embrace everything about them and cherish every moment I have with them. They are now young men and they are going to be set free in this challenging world soon. Thank you, God, for not letting me miss out on the lives of my two boys that are my most precious gifts from You. They now get to know a mom with a kind heart that is happier and has a strong faith; a faith I can only hope they truly embrace and live by someday. They now have an example in me they didn't have before.

I thank God often for redirecting my life that very dark, sad day… or so I thought was dark and sad. I thank Him for helping me find my wings and myself again. Heartbreak grew me and did not define me. I now celebrate the journey that took me from darkness to light. So many wonderful gifts have come from it. I choose to focus on the good and not the negatives that

I thank God for redirecting my life that very dark, sad day.

resulted from this journey. Pressing through the pain brought me to the good. I have embraced being a single woman raising two teenage boys. I continue to learn about myself and truly love who I am. I vow that my future relationships will have God at the center of them. I have learned to trust God and that he is in charge of my journey, not I. Now when I have times that I am worried or scared, I actually picture God's arms around me, and it gives me so much comfort and assurance. I am a child of God. He has my back and will always love me. I know there are many good things in my life that are yet to come because of God's grace.

With faith comes hope.

I now trust the journey because God is beside me, He always has been.

"I am free." These are the last words ringing out in the chorus of KRISTINA WARD's chart topping single, *"Be Free,"* from her debut album, *#UNFILTERED.* The lyrics perfectly describe an artist who's ready to liberate others. After a lifetime of service in many ways that didn't satisfy her longing for purpose, Kristina made the bold move to Nashville to start a music career. the providence of God was clearly being seen. The right friends, co-writers, and producers came together to allow her to fulfill a lifelong dream of putting her heart to song and sharing it with the world. Her music is the culmination and story of a young girl's journey to find her identity, belonging and acceptance in God. Freedom is ironically found in being bound to the right things, and as Kristina has fastened herself to God, her song will release others into this same truth.

Breakthrough

17

WALLS DOWN – LIFE UP

Kristina Ward

Have you ever found yourself in a place you swore you would never go again? Have you ever felt so much shame from that decision that it was crippling to you? Or so much pain your heart actually ached?

Flashes of memories flooded my mind. 'How could I be back at this place? How could I have let my guard down?'

The rushing sound of water flowed over me. The smell of coconut, humidity, and heat, surrounded me. As I collapsed to the steamy shower floor, sobbing uncontrollably, shame filled the air.

'I did it again, Lord. I did it again! Please forgive me!

Please . . . please . . . please forgive me!'

Lying there on that hot shower floor, there was no more running or hiding. The pain was too much to bear and I cried out Lord, "I can't live like this anymore, something has to change or I don't want to live anymore."

A runner, a stuffer, that's what they call me. It's all I've ever known, keeping myself so busy I never had to face the things I held so close to my heart. Hiding behind the masks of success, ministry, music, and perfection, I never allowed anyone to truly see the thing that has been

I've struggled with so much emotional baggage.

following me my whole life: a deep, dark black hole of loneliness in my heart. I've struggled with so much emotional baggage coming from a childhood of abuse. It had shaped me in ways I never imagined. On the outside, the bruises had healed. On the inside, they were still very much there. Years and years of neglect, rejection, and abandonment from the one who was supposed to love me, protect me, and give me a safe place to call home, left me longing. I was longing for something I never even knew I was longing for: a family! A support system of people that would love me for just me, and that I could for once count on.

Sadly, it has taken me up until last year to even realize this was the hidden piece I had been praying for years to be revealed to me; it was the key to my brokenness. All I could hear and see were the lies the enemy had been speaking into my life since I was a little girl. Lies that something was wrong with me. Lies that I was too much, broken, unlovable, and very much alone and that would always be the case. I had listened to the lies so long that I truly believed them. That is, until a year ago, when something happened and deep healing took place that changed my life forever . . . *a breakthrough*. It all started when I said yes to the call, the call to move to Nashville three years prior.

I knew if I was going to really walk in what God had called me to do, and for me to really minster to others, I was going to first have to face the demons of my past. It didn't take long into the move before He started shifting things, and I could tell my life was getting ready to change in ways I wasn't sure I was ready for. Within six months I was in full swing of my first album, writing, creating, and doing what I had always dreamed of. He started placing some of the most amazing people in my life, but there was one special sister in particular I felt drawn to. I couldn't put my finger on it other than I knew God had a very special friendship in store for us. She became close quickly and was able to reach me deeper than anyone has ever been able to reach, pushing past walls I didn't even know I had without me even realizing it. And, by the time I did, it was too late, because by then she was one of the rare ones I considered family.

It wasn't long before I started feeling all kinds of insecurities and fears over the friendship, scared to death that somehow I would be too much, and I would lose one of the few people I allowed to get close to me. The enemy played off of that so many times, causing pressure that should never be on a friendship. I became needy and codependent, which made it even worse. It's not a normal way for me to act with anyone; I have always had to be strong and independent, only letting people so close. But not with this one, and the more I tried to fix it or fight it, the worse I made it. I began to have drastic trigger moments from my past that would send me into depressions for days; on some occasions I thought I was losing it.

It was at this point I knew I needed more help than I could offer myself, so I sought out a Christian counselor to try and understand what was going on. There I began to see I was not losing it, but rather dealing with Post Traumatic Stress Disorder (PTSD). All the rejection and pain I stuffed as a child was surfacing and taking on a life of its own. I went through several treatments to help, but found that it only seemed to make my triggers worse.

They increased and became stronger; I even started having panic attacks. I would wake up in the middle of the night unable to breathe. My mind would race uncontrollably, causing months of sleepless nights. The stress began to also take a toll on me physically. I stopped eating, got down to a crazy low weight, and found it extremely hard to function in my day to day life.

But somehow, even in the midst of all this struggle, I still had faith and knew I had to keep pushing through. Thankfully during this time, the Lord brought someone in my path that was able to help me understand what was going on in my mind and body. Having come from a very similar background she was able to accept me exactly where I was at and, even more so, share how to help fix it. She had made it her life's work to understand the body and all of its responses; that kind of knowledge helped start the road of recovery.

This process was more than just an emotional and physical journey, it was a spiritual battle . . . a battle to take me out. I had lost who I was and pushed the one person I let in to her breaking point. She could no longer handle me, and all the lies once again flooded back in and proved to be true. I was too much, and unlovable. I started putting the walls back up. That's when I leaned into my guilt-laced, "I did it again," moments. Shutting out the world, and even the ones God sent me, was my go-to routine. Only this time it was so much more, I had hit my breaking point, a rock bottom moment, and I no longer wanted to live. The loneliness and pain had finally taken its last toll; and only He could reach me.

And that's when I heard a sweet, gentle, but greater voice step in; reminding me of a recent women's retreat I had attended and what He had spoken loud and clear.

"I need you to walk in your healing! I came that you may have life. By my stripes, you have been healed."

"All I need you to do is hear my voice, no matter what others say. Say yes to me, I am your safe place, your refuge; I will direct you and guide you into glory."

"Did you know dear daughter that your destiny is glory in me? I want you to begin to see yourself as glorious; I want you to see me as glorious, our relationship as glorious, and our future together as glorious; see our love and intimacy as glorious. I want that word to be so deeply ingrained in you that

you can't separate what it means from who you are! Because you are my daughter and you're destined for glory."

*Kristina's tattoo reminds her of **whose** she is!*

In total awe, I couldn't believe what I was hearing. That kind of love went straight to the core of who I was. Reminding me once again who I was, and, even more importantly, whose I was. I am the daughter of the King, and adopted into His family! I am enough, *never too much*, I am loved, and I am not alone!

Over the weeks and months to come, I began to see His mighty hand stepping in to restore all that was taken from me. He even used all the pain from this experience to birth an anointed new album called "Be Still". He began to breathe new life back into me, restoring what had been taken, and even restoring a friendship that was truly broken and turning it into something beautiful. He has shown me that I can lean into relationships that are God-honoring. And gave me a peace I've never known—for once my mind is at peace—my heart is full, and I am finally healed.

I am finally His.

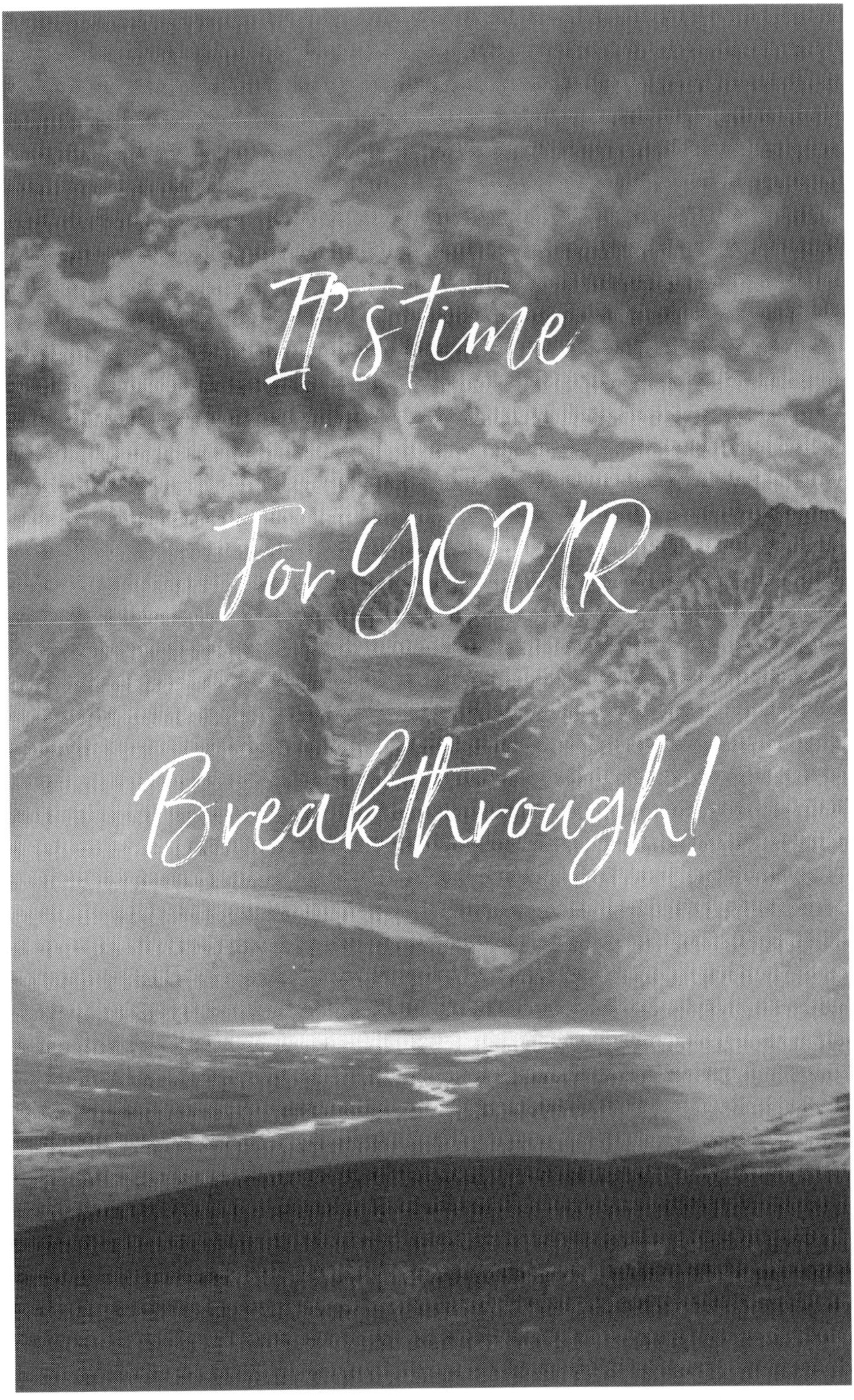
It's time
For YOUR
Breakthrough!

The Formula for Breakthrough™ is:

$$F \times T \times PR \times PT \times S^2 = BT!$$

How close are you to your breakthrough? Find out by answering these questions.

"F" is For Faith

1. Do I believe that no matter what happens in life, God is good and has GOOD things in store for me?

2. Do I believe that God's Word is true? (Psalm 119:160)

3. Do my actions and words line up with these beliefs?

4. Where do I get my identity and my worth from? What does God's Word say about me, my identity and my worth?

5. Do I believe what God says about me is the Truest thing about me?

6. Is my FAITH in Jesus Christ the foundation of my life and reflected by my obedience to Him?

7. Do I read and study the Word of God on a regular basis?

8. Do I pray for myself, loved ones and others on a regular basis?

9. Do I have a list of affirmations based on God's Word that I speak over myself on a regular basis?

10. What is one action I can take to improve my Faith walk?

11. Who might I need help from to make these changes?

"T is For

Truth

1. What things am I believing about myself or my circumstances right now that are limiting me? (Any statement that starts with "I can't because..." or "I could never" would be a huge clue! Others might be, "That will never work," or "That will never happen.")

2. What reality am I afraid to face? What's my reality check? (Are people who care about me telling me to wake up about something?)

3. Am I ignoring red flags about myself or others? If so, what are they?

4. Do I welcome truth in my life, or do I shy away from it?

5. What is one action I can take to face the Truth and come into the light?

6. Who might I need help from to make these changes? Who might walk me through facing my truth with gentleness and hope?

"PR" is For

Personal

Responsibility

1. What situation do I need to take some responsibility for? What is my part in the problem I'm facing?

2. What can I do better or different to change the outcome?

3. Who or what have I spent way too much energy trying to control? What is behind my efforts to control? Fear? What am I afraid of? Anger? What makes me so angry in this situation?

4. How will I make it right my wrongs and do things differently in the future?

5. Who do I need to let off the hook (stop blaming and trying to change them) as I look in my own mirror and keep my own side of the street clean?

6. What is one action I can take to take ownership over my choices in this situation?

7. Who might I need help from to make these changes?

"PT" is For

Proper Tools

1. What are some not-so-effective or even destructive tools I
    am still relying on to cope with my life?

2. How is the effectiveness of my current set of tools
    impacting my quality of my life and relationships? (Be
    specific.)

3. Am I satisfied with the level of effectiveness of my current
    set of tools?
    (Circle one:)   YES   NO

4. What are some books, people, resources or services that I
    currently have available to me but am not making use of?
    Who can point me to some effective resources if I have no
    idea where to begin?

5. What are some more helpful and effective tools or skills I might replace the old ones with?

6. What is one action I can take to get the new tools and skills I need to succeed?

7. Who might I need help from to make these changes?

"S^2" is For

Solid

Support

1. The following is a list of people I would consider high quality, trustworthy, "inner circle" people who I look to and can rely on for support, mentorship and guidance during my hardships:

2. The following is a list of people that I know bring me down, criticize me, take from me, manipulate me, are not honest, are not reliable, and are not working hard on their own growth and progress in life:

3. The above list of people who affect me negatively should not have intimate access to my heart and life and should not be in my inner circle:
(Circle one:)   TRUE   FALSE

4. The community support I currently have in place is (church, bible study, 12 step group, support group, group coaching, etc.):

5. The community support I lack right now is (name specific group you are not a part of that you feel led to participate in:)_____, and these are some available options for me to try:

6. What is one action I can take to strengthen the support in my life?

7. Who might I need help from to make these changes?

IT IS VERY IMPORTANT that you choose ONE area to focus your efforts first. Working on ONE thing until you've experienced some success before you move on to another increases your odds of overall success!

Make this commitment to yourself and to God today:

I WILL COMMIT TO WORK ON:

_____

_____

by doing this:_____

_____

and telling _____

about it for accountability as I work toward breakthrough.

To go from broken to BREAKTHROUGH, you must:

Keep the Faith,
Face the Truth,
Take Responsibility,
Get the Proper Tools
And have Solid Support
NOW is the time for your

Breakthrough!

These five factors for breakthrough will not fail you. Together, they have done MIRACLES in my life, heart, finances, marriage, family, relationships and health. I want you to see and understand that it is not because I'm special or favored or different than you… I spent YEARS of my life in total defeat. Until. Until God, who IS VERY SPECIAL, showed me how to put these five factors to work in my life without me even realizing it at the time!

"Breakthrough is guaranteed if there is enough light."

Sunday Adelaja

Invite The God Of Breakthroughs...

We know that the greatest breakthrough of all can occur right here in these pages. The good news of the Gospel is that we cannot only find ways through our struggles with Jesus, but we can invite Him to dwell in our hearts permanently, opening the way for breakthrough-after-breakthrough.

The promise, made by Jesus, for those who have been saved by grace through faith, is that saying "YES," to Him means that we will receive the Holy Spirit, the Spirit of breakthrough, from The God Of Breakthroughs!

Have you said "YES," to the free gift of salvation in Jesus Christ? If you do, you can today be assured of His breakthroughs in your life.

You are invited to pray the prayer below.

Begin your journey *today* toward a transformational, joyful, breakthrough-after-breakthrough life by inviting Him into your heart.

Father, I believe that your Son, Jesus, lived on this earth to ultimately die for me.

I know I've sinned; I've missed the mark many times and I cannot save myself.

I know that no amount of good deeds can wash me clean — but Your blood can!

Today, I choose to place my trust in the price you paid on the cross. I now turn from my own ways and toward You.

I ask you to make me new and fill me with your Holy Spirit today!

Thank You for dying for me and giving me the gift of eternal life.

Thank you for sending Your Holy Spirit to live in my heart and to guide my breakthroughs, now and always.

Amen

BECOME ONE OF THE FEW

In addition to monthly lessons, women's leadership, coaching, and retreats, The Fellowship Of Extraordinary Women (FEW) is proud to stand by these impactful, engaging, and True reads (with a "Big T"). Enjoy some of the many other inspirational titles from FEW International Publications. Most FEW books are sold on Amazon and almost all FEW authors are available to present to your church or organization. Refer to their websites listed in the biographies of this book. OR – reach out to FEW International Publications Founder and President, Kimberly Joy Krueger, at **www.kimberlyjoykrueger.com**.

Currently seeking women authors of all levels and experience who wish to have an extraordinary experiential writing journey in a book that glorifies God. Interested? You could be added to our list of dozens of #1 Bestselling Authors. Email: **Kimberly@thefewwomen.com**.

Made in the USA
Columbia, SC
05 December 2018